Tbilisi
Archive of Transition

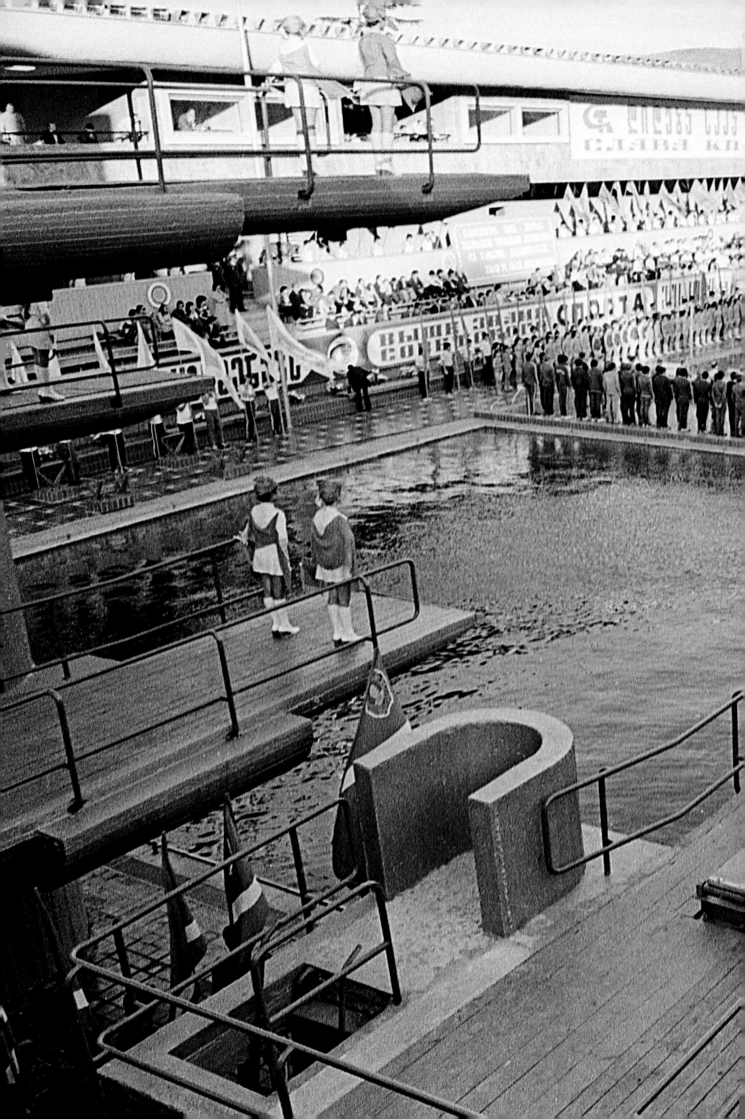

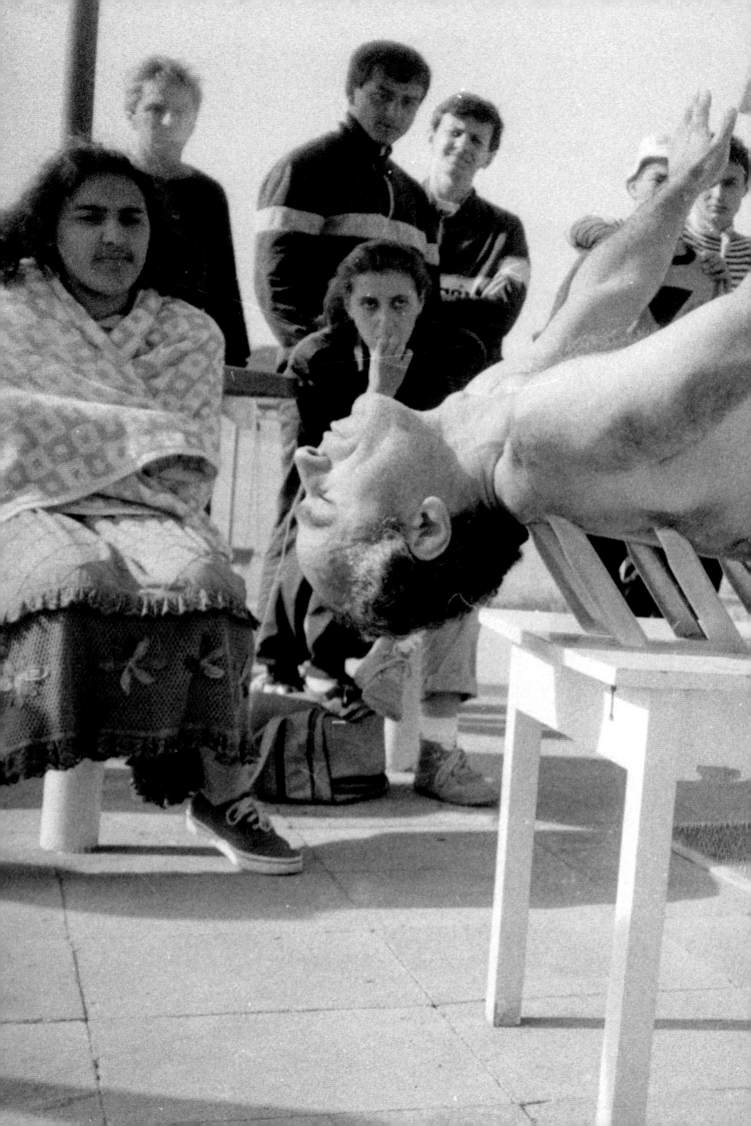

1   Two generations of microraions – or residential microdistricts – on the northern periphery of Tbilisi – Zghvisubani in the foreground with the expanse of the Gldani district in the background. The flayed central tower is home to refugees from the wars following the collapse of Soviet rule, and is locally known as ar ashenda – or »not finished, not constructed.« A vertical refugee settlement inhabits the shell of this Temka housing block.

2   Bus station at the amusement park Mtatsminda. On top of Mount Mtatsminda sit both the large Ferris wheel as well as the iconic television tower, two of the city's most prominent visual features. While tourists take the funicular to the top of the mountain, most of the locals prefer the yellow bus line.

3   Fare dodgers on a local bus line in 1993. Today's city planners consider the development of a functioning public transport system as one of the most important tasks for the city's future.

4   Aerial photograph of Varketili district from 1988. Across the USSR, standardized microraions – or micro districts – provided housing for a fast growing urban population. Today many of the flats are owned by their occupants, who have left their own highly personalized stamp on them. While this photograph shows a scant dozen cars, the Varketili of today is a site of lively bustle and congestion at street level.

5   Opened in 1978, Laguna Vere was one of the most important aquatic sports complexes in the Caucasus. The highly decorated brutalist building hosted national and international events, while at the same time being an important center for public recreation. In a familiar pattern, the complex was privatized in 2000 and was eventually shut down in 2014 as the new owners could not turn it into a profitable business. During the dramatic flooding of the River Vere in 2015 the building was severely damaged as mud and debris filled the former pool basin.

6   Soccer field in the backyard of housing towers on Nutsubidze Plateau.

7   Jemal Menteshahvili is demonstrating Raja Yoga in the Tbilisi Fitness Club in 1989.

8   The former Tbilisi Hippodrome is one of the city's largest green spaces. Once the site of horse races on the edge of the city, it soon became encircled by the growth of the Saburtalo and Vake districts. Over the past 20 years, the Hippodrome has seen significant development along its edges, but remains a vast green swath in the heart of the city. Subject to ongoing development pressures, the future of this de facto park remains unclear.

9   Tbilisi sports hall from 2011. Rugby, wrestling, and soccer were all part of a larger politics centered on the body. Sport and recreation were central to a Soviet narrative extolling the strength and vigor of the body politic, with many of the venues still in operation today.

10   Rooftop view from a hotel in 2011, across the topographically defined city.

11   Newspaper kiosk near Rustaveli Avenue and Republic Square (now Rose Revolution Square) in 1973. The Hotel Iveria rises above the trees as the then-tallest building in Tbilisi.

12   Funicular station near Turtle Lake. With its first cable car line opened in 1957, Tbilisi acquired a large and complex aerial transportation network over the next decades. Today the remains of abandoned station buildings are found throughout the city while plans to revive the cable car infrastructure are discussed by city planners and private companies.

13   In the mid-1990s the Avant-Garde Fashion Assembly was one of the most important platforms for fashion in the post-Soviet sphere. Its founder, Gela Kuprashvili, was 23 years old when he started the international festival in 1995 during the »dark years« of Georgian post-independence.

14   Former caravanserai in the old town of Tbilisi. Situated between Eastern Europe and western Asia, Georgia has always been an important bridge between the two continents. Numerous caravanserais developed to service the caravans that passed through this trade route. Though some of these roadside inns have been revitalized and host wine bars or museums, most houses still hide their history behind huge gated yards.

15   Tbilisi as seen from Turtle Lake, with upper Vake at the foot of the hill. Vake is one of the most expensive districts in Tbilisi and also the point where the city merges into the mountains. New building ground is hard to find as urban development comes crashing against its topographic limits.

In the Georgian language »Tbilisi« contains the word »heat«. This heat is an etymological witness to the hot springs that have their source at a particularly rocky bend of the Mtkvari River – springs that encouraged the original settlement of the city and that course through the geography of the old town to this day. Walking through the city, it is as if its streets are charged with the energy of this heat – reflecting off the walls of the houses and ricocheting off the rocky walls of the river. Built against sharp ridges and spread across high plateaus, Tbilisi demands conflicting interpretations. As much a topographic artifact as it is a cultural one, it is a place that carries its history deeply but that does not hesitate to discard its past selectively. Our received tropes of center/periphery, east/west, Europe/Asia, all come crashing down above these hot springs. It is a place of intensely lived contradictions, which you can always feel boiling under the surface.

In setting out to research the city's social, architectural, cultural, and historical dimensions, we were alert to the ways the city's contradictions are heightened at this particular moment. Over the past decade, Georgia has experienced an intense transformation that is particularly reflected in its capital – where ambitious building projects and increased foreign investment have led to a sense of constant transformation across the city. This transformation demands new discussions among the city's inhabitants and raises important questions: What is to be preserved and what is to be destroyed? What can be owned and what belongs to everyone? What do we want to remember and what can be forgotten?

With the *Archive of Transition*, we set out to record different dimensions and velocities of change within the city. We talked to artists and city planners, architects and activists, historians and cyberneticians, to understand what change means to all of them. While in our archive these interpretations sit next to each other on an equal register – like index cards in a file drawer – making a coherent book from this material suddenly creates new meanings, conclusions, and perspectives. In concluding our work we suddenly faced a question we had consistently deferred: Which Tbilisi do we want to show?

There's a saying that the archive isn't complete until the archiver is dead. Thus we don't consider this a finished book but more a snapshot of a city within a global age of transition. There's no reason why it shouldn't look entirely different tomorrow.

Archiving the Archive
Sebastian Pranz

The day before we started our work on the *Archive of Transition* the driver took us to the newly-rented office. The flat hadn't been in use for months, it was in the middle of the night and for some reason the electricity was dead. We stumbled through our pitch-dark apartment, searching through every room with nothing but a tea light. Ten hours earlier, heavy rain had caused the River Vere to break its banks and flood the city, taking not only cars, houses and roads with it but also destroying the fences of the nearby zoo. When we arrived, animals were roaming the streets of Tbilisi: a pack of wolves had to be shot in front of a kindergarten, a tranquilized hippo was being pushed through the streets, a construction worker was killed by a tiger and a penguin was picked up near the border with Azerbaijan. Our empty flat seemed like it may have been the perfect hiding place for one of them.

Zoos are archives for living creatures. Like the modern archive, the European zoo has its origin in the colonial expansion of the European empires during the 18th and 19th centuries. As soldiers were taking vast areas of land, scientists (and wannabe scientists) roamed the newly-conquered places gathering any kind of information about the foreign cultures. Back in Europe, private museums like the so-called »Wunderkammer« were filled with horns, shells and tusks, while zoos in Hamburg, Antwerp and Barcelona added live elephants, tigers, lions, apes and even humans from overseas to their collections. The inventory of the colonial archive soon became a representation of foreign places, feeding the western imagination and demand for exotica: »The soldiers and the administrators constructed objects of representation that became the reality of India,« said Indian scholar Gayatri Spivak of her home country.[1] The archive offered a perfect framework for the imperial thirst for knowledge as it reduced the complexity of cultural and natural realities to an inventory that could be stored and categorized. Or to put it more clearly, the archive answered the »necessity to acquire and order information about the new territories«[2] and was therefore in »the vanguard, not the rear, of the pursuit of colonial power.«[3]

Advertisement for a Völkerschau in Stelling, Germany in 1913. Like the modern archive, the European zoo has its origin in the colonial expansion of the European empires during the 18th and 19th centuries. In so-called »Völkerschauen« European zoos displayed not only animals but also humans.

The colonial archive illustrates that archives are more than passive containers. They define what is to be remembered and what to be forgotten. They construct and rewrite identities, they preserve and they erase data. When we started to work on the *Archive of Transition* we had the simple idea of building a database of places connected with the rapid social change taking place in Tbilisi. But we soon realized that talking about space in a city in transition is a highly political issue. During the three years of our research, historic buildings literally disappeared overnight, public ground turned into building sites and whole new districts emerged. This dynamic led to new questions: Who decides what is to be erased and what is to be preserved? Who has the power to add new points to a city's map? And to what extent is the transformation of a city discussed in the public discourse? In other words, our perspective shifted from the archive we were about to build to the *city being an archive in itself.*

It seems that Georgian society has always been in the middle of a transformation. Being of great geopolitical interest to many emperors over the centuries, this small country endured several phases of foreign domination before finally becoming part of the Soviet Union in the 20th

1 Spivak, G, *A Critique of Postcolonial Reason*, (Camebridge MA 1999), 203.
2 van Alphen, E, *Staging the Archive. Art and Photography in the Age of New Media* (London 2014), 41.
3 Ibid. One can also find the mutual connection between archiving and ruling in the 20th century. Ernst van Alphen argues convincingly that the genocide committed by the Khmer Rouge in Cambodia and the Holocaust where also preceded by the establishment of an archival organization turning human beings into numbered objects that could easily be ordered, observed and killed. (ibid., 193).

century. But when in 2003, after nearly 15 chaotic years of independence, the Rose Revolution took place, a new generation of politicians emerged who imagined Georgia as a country dissociated from its Soviet past, rapidly heading towards the future. Being well aware of the fact that Georgia had no significant natural resources, Mikheil Saakashvili's government started a new policy of attracting small and medium-sized companies from Europe to invest in Georgia. The narrative of a modernized Georgia spread with the message that the ministry welcomed every new business with low tax rates.[4] But this was only one side of the story. The drive for modernization left out the majority of Georgians living outside the capital, and didn't take into account the generation that had spent the first half of their lives in the Soviet era. In the context of a modernized Georgia, their pasts were being »rendered void«.[5]

Perhaps the greatest effect this paradigm shift had was on Georgia's capital. One does not have to read between the lines to see the stamp of modernization in the city: the spaceship-shaped new theater, the Public Service hall, the Peace Bridge or the 130-m-high Millennium Hotel that had just recently been constructed in the city center are only a few of the controversial projects of recent years. Many of the local populace perceives this building boom with growing displeasure. When in winter 2012 the city authorities sent workers to restore the historic Gudiashvili Square they were suddenly faced with a crowd of young Georgians who had organized an occupy camp to save the old buildings from demolition; in 2014 the *Guerilla Gardening* movement formed to save Vake Park, where public ground had suddenly been declared building land. And in 2015 it was the ambitious Tbilisi Panorama project, initiated by former Prime Minister Bidzina Ivanishvili, that has brought people out onto the streets.

At first glance, the civil disobedience may have been directed at the privatization of public land and the lack of a transparent city policy. But there's more to it. To understand the paradigm of modernization to its full extent, a case from outside Tbilisi may be instructive. In December 2014, workers blew up parts of the archaeological area of Sakdrisi, an ancient goldmine in south-eastern Georgia. The mine dated from 3000 BC and was a rare document of the Kura-Araxes, a civilization that existed between 3400 and 2000 BC, leaving no written records. The mine had been an archaeological site for ten years and had received cultural heritage status in 2006. Apart from precious artifacts like ancient mining tools and jewelry, the archaeologists found, of course, gold. This attracted people who had other interests than discovering new information about Georgia's ancient past. When in 2012 a new coalition led by businessman Bidzina Ivanishvili won the parliamentary election, a Russian mining company – and major investor in the Georgian economy – suddenly got a license to exploit the mine.[6] Non-parliamentary groups like *Green Fist* organized an occupation of the site while a Georgian/German team of archaeologists tried to broker a compromise between preserving and exploiting the mine. In the end, the company simply created its own facts on the ground and blew up the parts the mine that were of archaeological interest, so »further salvage work was pointless«, as the company's officials stated.[7]

The plans for Tbilisi Panorama, a luxury hotel complex sitting above the city's old town, led to ongoing protests among the capital's citizens. Already in its first stage, the project was criticized by historians who want to preserve Tbilisi's architectural character.

4 A good example is the German concrete manufacturer HeidelbergCement, praising the new market on its webpage: »In the coming years, Georgia expects that strong economic growth and heavy investment in the construction sector, especially in the development of infrastructure, to bring about a significant increase in cement and concrete consumption. In 2013, HeidelbergCement Georgia supplied cement and/or concrete to almost every major construction project in Georgia.« Accessed April 8, 2018, www.heidelbergcement.com.

5 See Katrine Bendtsen Gotfredsen who analyzes the story of a middle-aged woman from Gori. Bendtsen Gotfredsen, K., »Void Pasts and Marginal Presents: On Nostalgia and Obsolete Futures in the Republic of Georgia«, In Slavic Review 2014.
6 See the report of Democracy & Freedom Watch, accessed April 8, 2018, www.dfwatch.net/what-was-lostwhen-a-mining-company-destroyed-the-ancient-sakdrisi-site-38139.

The inventory of the colonial archive soon became a representation of foreign places, feeding the western imagination and demand for exotica. The image shows the »Musei Wormiani Historia« by Danish physician Ole Worm.

The power to set data (»Macht des Datensetzens«)[8] includes building streets, hotels, walls or other architectonic »data« in public space, in a way that can't be undone without leaving traces. If we can assume that a building is something that is of common interest because it is part of a shared, cultural memory, the opposite is also true: power includes the ability to erase this kind of data from the map. In this sense the confrontations that took place on Gudiashvili Square, in Vake Park or in far-away Sakdrisi can be understood as a struggle between contrary modes of representation: How should Georgia present its present and past and how does it deal with the contradictions that occur between them? How is built memory in the city representative of what Georgia is today and who defines this identity? Who does the city belong to and who is telling its stories?

One week after the tragic incident, authorities claimed that all of the missing animals had been found. But officials also admitted that in the flood of mud, dirt and water it was hard to get a clear picture. Nevertheless, the tigers and lions that strolled the streets of Tbilisi have become part of the city's memory. They will reappear from time to time on the surface of the pool of narratives in the city. This archive is wild! Nobody will ever fully tame it.

7   Ibid.
8   According to German sociologist Heinrich Popitz. Popitz, H., *Phänomene der Macht: Autorität – Herrschaft – Gewalt – Technik* (Tübingen 1986), 107.

Sea

Wato Tsereteli and
Jesse Vogler

On November 4th, 1951, the water came Families gathered on the grassy slopes – dressed in their weekend best, carrying stoppered bottles of red wine and glasses. The men wear hats, the women scarves, to protect against the blustery, late-autumn winds that still scold the grass. Bulbous hoods of GAZ cars sit neatly like beetles just above the elevation of the spillway. The punctuated silhouette of people gives way to a scattering of strained trees in the sheltered valley, where the arc of a river maps the folding-back of the contours. Beyond the river is Tbilisi, cloaked in the backdrop of ridges.

All await the water. They were invited here, in a recapitulation of an antediluvian pageant. A group of people standing along the level earthwork gives way to the descent of four men walking across the edge of the flats. Two sit, holding their knees, facing the absent water. While two stand facing each other, marking the future littoral. Others, always paired, follow the neat arc of the road and the engineered lines of the embankment.

On November 4th, the water came It left the skies months ago – when it last rained in April. It has been stored 65 kilometers away, in a deep mountain valley, in a place called Sioni. There, the sharp level of an earthen dam captures the potential energy of an entire geo-hydro-political system, where the dreams of Soviet agriculturalists, the smells of fecund deserts and wet dirt, are stored.

But the water is no longer there. It has made its way for several days down the limestone bottoms of the River Iori. Past Kudro. Past Bochorma. Past Sasadilo. Toward Ujarma, King Vakhatang Gorgasali's 5th-century stone fortress, the second capital of Georgia until the 8th century – here it is held in the Iori reservoir at Otaraani until today.

On November 4th, the water came It takes 16 hours for the gravitational pull on the water to bring it from the Iori reservoir to here. Engineers drew their levels across the Iori plateau, across the Shiraki Plain, under mountains, and through 89 kilometers of channel to the Samgori valley. They call it the Zemo-Samgori Canal – the upper canal of the three hills. It is Georgia's largest drainage and irrigation system – its extents reaching to the arid Azeri border.

The water folds its way through the concrete-lined trapezoidal canal, blue and swift. Through the village of Saakadze, through the village of the disgraced warrior rehabilitated by Stalin, where it drops 150 meters from the flat plateau to the river valley below. Down through a pair of welded steel pipes to turbines that supply electricity to the airport and an abandoned fur coat factory. Past the new chicken farms and past the model state-farm to the closed basin beyond.

Where once there was dry grass, low bushes, lizards, mice, quail, and *mimino* – the sparrow hawk – comes the rush of water. Following the water emerge docks. Boats. The *Golden Fleece Youth Camp* and the Iori tourist hotel. A cool-blue lake in the yellow brown of August. What else could the hot, dusty city ask for? The chalk blue of the water betraying its calcite course. One lobe: smaller, shallower. The other: larger, deeper, darker. The Zemo-Samgori Canal cascading in a fierce, three-tiered-ziggurat of a channel into the sea.

39

40

In the summer of 1951, families were invited to the dry Samgori basin perched above the city to watch the Tbilisi Sea be filled with water.

To the Tbilisi Sea   We call it a sea. But it is only a sea by relation. There is no salt in this water to leave its chalky residue as it evaporates in the hot, rainless air. It is only as a proxy for the three small, milky lakes that used to dot this basin after a storm that this reservoir becomes a sea.

A sea by simile   But before the turquoise sea filled its sere band of hills, there were three briny, *mlashe* lakes that dotted the basin – Avlabari, Kukia, Ilguiani. Here, in the early 20th century, visionary Georgian polymath and statesman Nico Nicoladze envisioned the three salty lakes transformed into a cascade of interconnected, nourishing pools. He had a plan to bring water to the plateau above the city to catalyze a change in

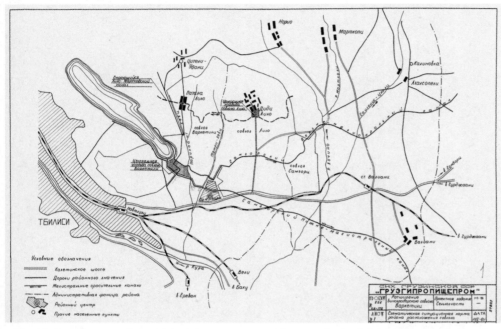

Map of the Tbilisi Sea and the Zemo-Samgori canal system. Also included are a patchwork of new agricultural villages arranged to capitalize on the newly irrigated land.

climate, a change in atmosphere, a transformation of the sour and dry airs in the city. A theory that water would beget more water. That the sea would purify the air and that its thermal mass would store the city's heat, just as it stored water for the cucumbers.

　　And he was right. The city's temperature dropped an average of 4 degrees following the construction of the sea. Fruit orchards and grapevines are made to grow where before not even the hardiest of grasses made it through the summer months un-desiccated.

On November 4th, the water came   People were invited to the high Samgori plateau above the city, to bear witness to an experiment in socio-economic ecologies. To leave their flats and watch the sandstone and clay basin slowly fill with water from the foothills of the Caucasus. At first the water is swift – carving a path in the dry basin dirt. But after the initial and irreversible diversion, the flow slows. It takes seven days to fill the sea. Over 31 million cubic feet of water, covering 250 hectares, transferred through lines and channels to the dust-dry basin above the city.

　　The once denuded banks are made to grow walnut, sequoia, spruce, and Italian pine trees – providing shelter for a quiet Tbilisi yacht club and the occasional pheasant flying heavily from tree to tree. The south bank generates a cornerstone of the Soviet planned economy – a state farm, the Varketili *meurneoba*. Here new varieties of fruit trees were subject to the even newer technology of pesticides, as the state farm formed a crystalline spatial structure of the managed economic system in which it was situated.

The mountain water does not find its terminus in the sea; it powers on, the battery for a vast irrigation system that tacks its way down-gradient from the Samgori Valley toward the Jandara Reservoir straddling the Georgian/Azeri border. Along the way, a 350 kilometer-long network of primary and secondary canals feed water to a patchwork of productive agricultural fields, supplying Tbilisi with its central food source.

But in the years of political and material transition, marked notably not so much by sabotage as by neglect, this irrigation network fell into disrepair. The territorial system of managed hydrologies and distributed state farms clogged in the last mile by disrupted concrete channels and stopped culverts. Chunks of concrete flumes were scattered across the landscape, which was made discontinuous. Aqueducts slumped, yielding to gravity.

But the sea remains. The boats are mostly gone. People no longer cluster along its shores but scattered in small groups around its littoral contour. Families take refuge from the still-sharp sun in the shadow of their cars, the occasional cow wandering to the lake for a drink of its milky waters. The sea perches there, charged with the potential energy pent up at the heart of its hydraulic diagram.

Once constructed, the Tbilisi Sea was a regular destination in a broader Soviet health culture that included a network of sanatoria and springs. Here, children play at the Golden Fleece Youth Camp.

Walking Through Betlemi

Nato Tsintsabadze
and Meghan O'Neill

Walking through Betlemi Quarter can feel a bit like discovering a secret garden from a past century. This part of the medieval town sits above the rest of Old Tbilisi and is geographically sheltered by the Sololaki ridge. From the community-garden area in front of the Upper Betlemi Church, visitors can look out at Tbilisi from a close, comforting vantage point. From this distance it's also possible to see the neighborhood and city below – even the Caucasus Mountains are in range. There is an intangible charm to the Betlemi Quarter that exists alongside many built cultural landmarks. This warm atmosphere is due in part to a fundamental *genus loci*, or spirit of place, but is also, and importantly, due to the activities of community members who work to maintain this spirit.

Scattered throughout the district are multiple examples of vernacular Tbilisi housing types from the 17th to 19th centuries. In addition, different religious buildings from the 5th century coexist in close proximity to one another. For example, Upper Betlemi Church, one of Tbilisi's first churches established by King Vakhtang Gorgasali in the 5th century, is only meters away from a pre-medieval Zoroastrian Fire Temple, or *Ateshgah*. The initial Upper Betlemi Church structure dates from the 5th century; however, several churches were built directly on this site over time. These buildings are fundamental to the fabric of the Betlemi Quarter, with its horizontal terraces and vertical street-stairs

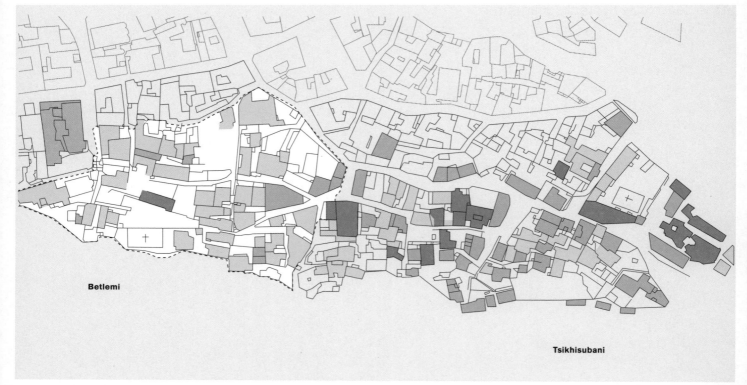

Betlemi

Tsikhisubani

connecting the district to the rest of the town. Such features have attracted architects, art historians, and conservators on a national and international scale.

The Georgian National Committee of the International Council on Monuments and Historic Sites (ICOMOS Georgia) began the community-based regeneration process for the Betlemi Quarter in 2001. Initially, in 1999, this team of architecture and art history specialists focused on conserving physical sites located within Betlemi. They marveled at individual stones, plaster, and other tangible relics from centuries ago.

A map by the International Council on Monuments and Historic Sites (ICOMOS) highlights the results of the so-called rehabilitation project »New Life of Old Tbilisi« undertaken by Tbilisi City in 2006–2012. The majority of the historic buildings were replaced with imitations during the process.

▨ Historic building
▨ Modern building (second half of 20th–21th c.)
▨ Building dismantled within the Project – »New Life of Old Tbilisi«. Majority of these buildings were replaced with historic imitations.

However, this fascination alone was unable to move their conservation project forward. They had to look beyond the artifacts themselves to the entire environment, and particularly to collaborations with the community who lived there in the present moment.

Every community consists of many individuals. Some residents of Betlemi Quarter were reluctant to participate in conservation efforts at first. Some still remain uninterested. At the time there was a general mistrust towards any organizations or groups left over from the Soviet period. The project team tried to approach this vulnerable and multiethnic community with sensitivity. They held community meetings and shared plans with total transparency. With funding for the Conservation Plan coming from the UNESCO Cultural Heritage Division and the Norwegian Ministry of Foreign Affairs, the Betlemi project team trained locals on conservation techniques and offered paid jobs during the project. The team gained trust and support by creating job opportunities, improving infrastructure services, and advocating for the preservation of the historic environment of the neighborhood. They also set up the Betlemi Quarter Information Center as a place where people could share their concerns and ideas. This meeting spot was instrumental for the project team and the community to work together.

In addition to being a significant community meeting place, the Betlemi Quarter Information Center was also an innovative and relevant reuse of a heritage building. The Center was set up in one of the oldest tower-dwellings of Tbilisi. This building is part of a small cluster of defense towers that greet visitors at the top of the renovated street-stair entrance to the Betlemi Quarter. Once inside, visitors are met with a comfortable community space with a palpable history. Some of the architectural details preserved in the Information Center include exposed medieval mortar, narrow staircases built into a wall, preserved wooden support beams, and an inexplicable pagan fertility symbol carved into the wall.

Despite initial setbacks in working with the community, some locals with exceptional skills and a passion for conservation stood out as leaders. Chito, a local craftsman, received conservation training from the project team at the beginning of the revitalization project. Many craftsmen like Chito, with newly acquired conservation skills and delight in their paid project, found the energy to improve their own historic homes in the neighborhood.

The Ateshgah rehabilitation project was the pinnacle of community involvement in the Betlemi project. Arguably the oldest building in Tbilisi, the Ateshgah tells a story of how various religions coexisted and followed in succession to one another in the historic city. In the temple there is a base of crudely cut rock, which scholars argue was used by pagans as a place of worship. A Zoroastrian place of worship was most likely built onto this layer. Afterwards, more interventions were done with different materials to convert the temple into a mosque. Chito and other local craftsmen worked to restore an old, non-functional staircase up to the Ateshgah and conserve these intricate historical layers inside the structure. Chito, along with his family, maintains the Ateshgah without any help from the city. They occasionally open the doors for visitors.

Betlemi's transition was the result of ten years of slow, considered change. Instead of being polished or commercialized overnight, the space transformed naturally as a community project. The Betlemi Quarter Revitalization Plan has not received funding since 2011; however, revitalization continues thanks to skilled craftspeople and the project's strong relationship within the community. Another way the project survives is through private support. The project team is able to consult with private clients interested in restoring their properties. In this way, community craftsmen receive more paid opportunities. Alongside these and other details, residents work to maintain the community garden, introduced as part of the Betlemi project, independently of the city.

Since 2010, every 17th of May, the community celebrates the Betlemi Festival on the terrace near the Upper Betlemi Church. The project team leads heritage walks around the quarter to raise awareness, demonstrating how a successful conservation project can function within the community. This is how the spirit of place survives amidst rehabilitation. Yet this renovation success story is not typical of current practices in historic Tbilisi. Certain areas that have undergone rehabilitation now

come across as flat and devoid of charm – yet tourists continue to flock to these areas. This is why heritage advocacy groups protest against development plans that are rushed, commercial, and ill-considered.

For example, since 2007 heritage activists have urged the city to consult with experts before starting any rehabilitation projects at Gudiashvili Square. Located just below the Betlemi Quarter, Gudiashvili Square is another medieval center in Old Tbilisi. This beloved area rests

An extract from the conservation plan shows Gudiashvili Square and its environs.

- Early 19th c.
- Mid 19th c.
- Late 19th c.
- 19th c. with layers from 17th c.
- 19th c. with layers from 18th c.
- Late 19th c. on old foundation.
- Turn of the 20th c.
- Early 20th c.
- Late 20th c.
- 21th c.

upon a network of intricate archaeological layers from the 17th and 18th centuries. The boundary line of the Gudiashvili Square project area runs across Dadiani Street and is built upon Tbilisi's medieval city wall. In addition to the medieval fabric of the site, buildings within Gudiashvili Square are symbolic of Tbilisi's cultural heritage. Members of the public were deeply upset when a development company circulated plans to demolish major historic buildings on the Square and crudely transform the iconic Blue House at 2 Gudiashvili.

This plan to transform the Blue House was part of a larger proposal to commercialize Gudiashvili Square with a network of new, glassy storefronts. Locals felt that their public space was under attack and their city's heritage was at risk. After these plans were shared on Facebook many young people mobilized in protest. An NGO known as Tiflis Hamkari was particularly active, as were different artist collectives and individuals. Young people felt as though a crucial space was being taken from them. Yet in the face of this devastating news, the protests were fun and creative events that brought people together. Every weekend, those with a passion for Tbilisi's heritage arranged festivals with music, food, and art. As a response, the city's plans to commercialize this historic community space came to a halt.

Following the halt of demolition, the city authorities enlisted ICOMOS Georgia to come up with a conservation plan for Gudiashvili Square to maintain its sense of place. In addition to the conservation guidelines, the conservation plan includes recommendations for implementation through a participatory approach to ensure multiple stakeholder involvement – like local community, heritage advocacy groups, etc. And just recently, in March of 2018, the Tbilisi City Hall held a public presentation at the square and announced a launch of the new rehabilitation works with investment of 50 million GEL of public funds. Due to the extreme visibility of the case and the long history of civic protest, the mayor has invited heritage experts and the wider community to monitor the process and promised to ensure collaboration and transparency. As the lessons of the Betlemi Quarter remind us, cultural heritage is more than just the sum of a collection of buildings, but is woven into a city's social fabric.

Formula Tbilisi
Wato Tsereteli

If you consider a creative product a field with multiple polarities, then Tbilisi is definitely an artwork. Wherever you come from, you recognize something in this city: something that is familiar to you. This something is likely evident in the architecture, the landscape, the people and their appearance. But who are these people and what language do they speak?

If you imagine history extending below your feet, vertically, you certainly fall into a deep hole. Somewhere, 5,000 years ago, you would hear an archaic, proto-Kartvelian language spoken here. A long memory, an autonomous language, and a mixed southern spirit, results in a strong identity … If you still don't know the origins of your language and ethnic background, but you find in the national museum the 6000 BC clay vessel with grape reliefs, your ego accelerates 10cm above reality.

The immune system of this society lies in the polyphony of its ambitions – a polyphony nicely shown in the film *The Way Home* by Alexander Rekhviashvili. Here, three protagonists meet on a field heading to expel an enemy. After a short discussion each of them chooses a different direction, a different route, to approach the enemy and to meet at the rendezvous point. This strategy of disorientation, of anti-homogeneity, suggests the active engagement of many individuals – individuals acting on their own toward a common goal. It is an interesting approach to collective action, a mechanism of diffuse identities.

How to be heard in a society where every other person is pretending to be an aristocrat, a king, and all of these multiple »kings« have different perspectives? This predicament stands in counterpoint to another component of the field: the unusual history of the peaceful co-existence of many religions and ethnicities over thousands of years. This loud sentence is not a simple cliché, but an historical fact.

It's remarkable that in Tbilisi's main mosque Shia and Sunni pray together, while the big synagogue, a liberal congregation, sits just 500 meters away. Tbilisi does not remember pogroms of any kind. This is the paradox for which there is so far no explanation: that in a place that encourages contrasting worlds – between Christianity and the Orient, between European and Soviet, between tolerant and individualist – there is a productive rather than destructive contradiction.

The 1954 Extension   Behind noisy Rustaveli Avenue, towards the hill of the holy mountain, in other words in the very center of Tbilisi, is a small, quiet, and concealed street – a street much like Georgia is a country. In the early days of the Soviet era the street was named after Karl Liebknecht; then in the 1990s it was renamed Perkhuli-volk Dance Street; and since the liberalization of 2000 it has been known as Solomon Zaldastanishvili Street.

On this street is a house built before 1880 out of 19cm×19cm bricks. These bricks are simply called old, or square, bricks. There were various sizes, from 18×18cm to 22×22cm, and there were dozens of brick manufacturers in Tbilisi at that time. Asked about the origin of these bricks and whether we should call them Asian bricks, Maia Mania, one of the most knowledgeable scholars of architecture in Georgia, answered: »No, these are not Asian bricks, they were used in Byzantium, too …« Bricks and lime create a combination of building materials that is flexible,

48

and that deals easily with earthquakes. We have had plenty of tremors over the past 25 years, and they have not damaged the house at all.

In 1954, an extension was built on this historical house that basically served as a staircase and added kitchens on two floors. The staircase is especially interesting, full of niches and extra built-in spaces. In the mezzanine of the staircase there is a small window, 18cm wide and 45cm high.

It happens that in this house, without any awareness of the century, the geography, the culture, or the city, I was born.

From early childhood, the frozen early 80s, I remember the practice of being put in an old, dark-green, Soviet minibus and taken out on »expeditions.« I would join a group of people who went to certain architectural monuments and did field work there – measuring, taking photographs, identifying structural problems, etc. Sometimes we drove to the remains of a Zoroastrian temple near the village of Kavtiskhevi – a site far from center that even now remains relatively unknown. If you go to the upper level of this half-ruined temple, minimally restored, you have a 360-degree view of a land that, for me, recalls Mesopotamia. Another of our expeditions would take us somewhere in the forest to visit a lone, 11th-century cross-cupola church. Again we measured, took photographs, then sat on the grass and had food – we were all tired. »Cross-cupola construction is very complicated,« my grandmother told me.

Now, I recognize that this house in the center of Tbilisi is an archive and also a bit of a museum. My grandparents, who always took me on these expeditions, happened to be art historians and restorers. Both strong personalities, they worked together: studying, restoring, and publishing books about Georgian architecture from antiquity through 18th and 19th century Tbilisi housing typologies.

The archive contains around 40,000 medium-format negatives depicting architecture from the 1940s till the end of the 1980s, architectural drawings, diaries, paintings, and graphics. As my background is in photography, I first dealt with the photo archive. The images are seemingly scientific: they primarily focused on architecture. But of course one cannot photograph only buildings, the photographs also capture people and the landscape around them.

I am trying to work with the archive carefully and will hopefully make it publicly accessible soon. It is not the easiest task, because how do you reassemble the existing archive into a new body open for public access? All the material should be digitized and conserved … I guess that art can contain the archive in itself …

A special part of the archive is material on Tbilisi, including material for a book published by my grandfather, Vakhtang Tsintsadze, in 1958, about housing in Tbilisi. The houses he studied, measured, drew, and photographed, later became guidelines for listing those houses as cultural heritage.

Standing back on the mezzanine of the old house in the center of Tbilisi, in the middle of the staircase, in the 1954 extension made by my grandfather, and looking through the small window trying to see the street, I was taken by the sudden idea that this small window was a message that my grandfather put into the building. It is definitely from another time and space. I understood that this tiny aperture corresponds with one that might be found in a medieval castle, where small windows were made to observe the immediate environment and to be ready for defense in case of an attack.

Tbilisi Vertical   In a dream, I once said to myself: »By chance, you have precious knowledge of the inner workings of Tbilisi; subjective, but containing information known by probably less than one percent of the city's inhabitants. So why don't you do something with it?«

So from this old house in the center of Tbilisi, and with the excursions of my grandparents as my guide, I set out to share this knowledge through the format of the walk. But following my practice as an artist, the walk had to challenge every aspect of being a guide in the city, including the financial side.

Concerning logistics: a short email, sms, or phone call is enough to fix the meeting place, and the duration of a walk can be adapted. The tour is a synthetic experience, in the sense that the plot is interrupted during the walks and interspersed with narrative … The plot of the tour is a rauella in itself …

After years of rethinking this city through these walks, excursions, and dwelling, I came upon a very simple idea: to turn this history of peaceful cohabitation into a future orientation and to initiate a peace platform in Tbilisi. I propose to call this platform the »Tbilisi Method« – a place for international peace talks and conflict resolution, with the sublime participation of the thermal springs.

1 Archeology of the Present

1
Archeology of the Present

1
Archeology of the Present

Archeology of the Present

Archeology of the Present

Archeology of the Present

This collection of photographs of Old Tbilisi is part of the Rusudan Mepisashvili and Vakhtang Tsintsadze Memorial Archive. Rusudan and Vakhtang were art historians and specialists in the restoration of Georgian architecture. In 1941 they co-founded the Institute of the History of Georgian Art, and from the 1930s until the 1980s were actively involved in theoretical study and publishing as well as the material conservation and restoration of pre-Christian and Christian architecture in Georgia. During the civil war of 1992, the building of the Institute of History of Georgian Art was burned down completely, and the entire archive was destroyed. After this loss, the archive of Rusudan Mepisashvili and Vakhtang Tsintsadze increased immensely in historical value. In addition to the roughly 40,000 photographs depicting Georgian architecture from the 1930s to 1993, the archive contains architectural drawings, scientific diaries, situational paintings, and other precious material – selections of which are shared here in print for the first time. At the moment the archive is in the process of being made public and in the near future anyone interested in the history of Georgian art will have the opportunity to use it for research.

Tbilisi Cosmopolis
Zaal Andronikashvili

I had an argument with a friend a while ago. He happened to be strolling in Tbilisi on Aghmashenebeli Avenue (Plekhanov Street during the Soviet times and Michael's Street in the time of the Russian Empire, where a colony of Swabian settlers was established in the early 19th century. Pushkin visited it and surprisingly disliked the German beer). He counted eleven Turkish flags during his walk – all raised above Turkish restaurants – and was apprehensive the area might soon resemble Kreuzberg (a »Turkish« quarter in Berlin). I am going to neither accept this line of argument nor try to explain why Kreuzberg is indeed an exemplary neighborhood. I would rather dig deeper into the subject as to why a reaction to something »foreign,« in this case »Turkish«, has become possible in a big city at all.

What is the mechanism that allowed him to transpose »foreign« as an equivalent to »dangerous«? To me, the reason lies in Tbilisi turning into a provincial town during the last ninety years. I will try to explain why Tbilisi, to my mind, is a provincial town now and why it was not ninety years ago, when it still was a *cosmopolis*. To explain the distinction between this bizarre world-city type and an ordinary polis (a city-state) or a megalopolis (a super-city) I will have to make a detour through a series of Greek and Roman attitudes toward the city and the specific reconfiguration of identity and limits that they make possible.

The difference between a *polis* and an *oikos*, a city and a household, is a distinct marker of a Greek city-state. A household and a city are based on different kinds of order. While a polis is made up of *oikoi* – households, families, etc. – the city also forms a separate space where men (for women were excluded from political and civic life) are transformed and acquire the distinct status of citizen. However, a city performs this transformation by first transforming a man to an individual (a citizen) and in the process of this transformation making him into a social animal, a *zoon politikon*. The city effects this transformation through the production of citizen-space. It creates places such as the agora or the theater where the private is transformed into the common, the social, and the public. This is the line of thought I would like to follow.

The theater in Athens, where three tragedies and one comedy were performed at the festivals of Dionysus, was one such place of transformation. A tragic plot does not only *narrate* change from good fortune to bad, but *performs* a transformation of its protagonists (men and women, since tragic plot is more inclusive than ancient polis). An example will clarify my point. In Sophocles' *Antigone*, the chorus addresses Antigone who is condemned to be buried alive by Creon for giving her brother, Polyneices, a proper burial against the will of Creon, her uncle and the King of Thebes:

> »It is a great thing for a woman who has died to have it said of her that she shared the lot of the godlike in her life, and afterwards, in death.«[1]

As this suggests, the heroine (or hero) of a tragedy differs from other mortals insofar as the heroine goes beyond the human and approaches the divine while maintaining her humanity by way of her very mortality. This is why her only course for transformation lies through pain, doom, and death.

---

[1]   Translation: Sir Richard Jebb

61

The theater is a place where a spectator, who was not so fortunate as Antigone or Oedipus, observes a tragedy with pity and fear (*eleos kai fobos*) in order to purify himself; and through this viewing gains access to the experience of transformation. The theater – and it shares this quality with the agora – is a place where a human, as a result of extreme effort, is able to go beyond his limits, to become more than he is, while maintaining his humanity; to be simultaneously the »I« and more than the »I«. »Identity«, on the contrary, stresses a certain sameness between I and I, and does not allow transformations of the kind outlined above.

I will give one more example, this time from political religion: a Roman *triumphator* who had excelled in a war, was required, upon returning to his city, to be unarmed when crossing the boundary of Rome. The city honored him with almost divine veneration and an exceptional ceremony; for example by dressing him as a statue of Jupiter. As the *triumphator* was about to sacrifice two snow-white oxen to Jupiter, he would take an oath, which relativized his exceptional honors: he vowed to never attempt or desire to become a king in Rome. However, later Roman emperors permanently appropriated the exceptional honors of the *triumphator*. The Roman triumph, just like the tragedy, was another reflection of the fact that a human, as a result of a great effort, can surpass his own humanity and go beyond his limits.

These examples from the Greek polis and Roman triumph suggest that a city is a spatial embodiment of a human's ability to become »universal« without losing his particularity – to surpass himself, to transcend himself. A city actually creates spaces suitable for the process of transformation.

But the city not only *effects* this transformation of subjects: a city is also capable of transforming and transcending *itself*. Here, I do not refer to changes that a city naturally undergoes with the passage of time. Rather, I suggest a city is capable of transcending its own geographic/temporal situation. While it is true that a city is objectively bound to one place, there are ways in which the city exceeds this situation. Here, it may be productive to recall the Roman cynic Seneca, writing in a tragedy about a woman, Medea, who Georgians usually consider a compatriot:

> »All bounds have been removed, cities have set their walls in new lands, and the world, now passable throughout, has left nothing where it once had place: The Indian drinks of the cold Arazes, the Persians quaff the Elbe and the Rhine. There will come an age in the far-off years when ... Thule not be the limit of the lands.« [2]

We should be careful not to mistake this for an early description of globalization. The chorus utters these words when reflecting upon the past: there were times when everyone was subject to the same law, bound to the same place, and buried wherever he had been born. The Argo, on the other hand, ignored the autochthonous law and thus ruled the sea. In other words, what we nowadays call globalization sprang from the first human who chose to leave his native land and go travelling. The story of the Argonauts is the story of how humans violated the autochthonous law, how they surpassed themselves, and thus is an example of topographic transcendence.

2 Translation: Frank Justus Miller

Globalization is the history of a global village – the provincialization of the world. This is not my subject. I would like to tell another story, about the city being able to change the fundamental order just like a human and hence transcend its roots and become universal without ceasing being particular. This is the city that Seneca spoke about as having set its walls in new lands. A cosmopolis is a city gone travelling. Keep in mind, however, that travelling would not mean, for example Tbilisi setting off to far-away lands, settling down somewhere near the seashore (this would be a model of a colony). A city gone travelling does not possess a steady, fundamental order – national or imperial. It does not submit itself to any power whatsoever, even when a power might reside within a city. Rather, the city creates a parallel space, free from power, an atopic space where the private becomes the public; the particular turns into the universal.

In our time, every city lies within a state (be it a nation-state or not); and yet, New York, London, or Berlin are much more than just national cities. They transcend their national self, becoming plural and international cities. Here, »international« is not an antonym of »national«. These cities are capable of transforming a newcomer not exactly into a native, but into one who belongs equally to the city. This would not produce an American, an English person or German. Rather, people who live there are New Yorkers, Londoners and Berliners – if not eternally, at least for some time. This happens without any integration policy whatsoever, but simply occurs through the qualities of transformation that the city possesses. This is precisely the transformation described by the German philosopher Walter Benjamin in his *Arcades Project*, a work of psycho-spatial insight dedicated to the city of Paris. The title and the fragmented structure of the book seems to me the best manner in which the *atopy* of the cosmopolis can be described. A city does not have any internal, eternal order to it. Rather, anybody, as a citizen or visitor, creates his or her own order by the routes they draw in the city.

To return now to Tbilisi, one of the many who drew his own route through this city was Sayat-Nova, an 18th-century poet and musician. Armenian by descent, he wrote in three, and according to some even five, languages – though most of his poetry is in Turkish. More than a century passed after his death when Sergo Parajanov, a Tbilisian film director of Armenian descent, looked back on Sayat-Nova as his own forerunner and dedicated his groundbreaking film, *The Color of Pomegranate* (1969), to him. Parajanov was one of the protagonists of the disorderly-order, the atopy inherent to Tbilisi. As such, it is apt that his statue in Tbilisi does not actually stand on the ground (as all decent statues would) but rather hangs in the air. Additionally, the website of Tbilisi City Hall, for unknown reasons, lists a photo of the statue under the name of »Bacchus, God of Wine.« I do not really think Parajanov would have minded such confusion. Does hanging in the air mean that the Armenian actually failed to set his roots deep in the Georgian national soil? Or is it an implication that he, as the true symbol of Tbilisi, cannot have any roots at all – as a city gone travelling is, in fact, a city without roots?

While I may be creating a mythology here, Tbilisi, for a couple hundred years, was such a *cosmopolis*. Whether big or small does not really matter; as irrespective of size, a cosmopolis is a cosmopolis. Due to its history, Tbilisi was not just a Georgian city. For years, Georgians were a minority living alongside others: Arabs, Persians, and Armenians. The place, as the meeting point for many cultures and ethnic groups, shaped the profile of the city. To be a Tbilisian was to transcend the national. One was no longer Georgian, Armenian or Persian. One became Tbilisian. The standard clarity of national identity was muddied – where mothers and fathers, grandmothers and grandfathers, were of mixed nationalities and faiths, and all spoke three or four languages. »Here,« writes the hero of Aka Morchiladze's *Flight over Madatov Island and Back*, »the Shia and the Sunni are brothers.«[3]

We must imagine that in this cosmopolis, even the acoustics of the city were different. This is what we hear, in the form of »oriental« music, in the background of *Falling Leaves* (1966) and *There Once Was a Singing Blackbird* (1970) – two masterpieces by Otar Iosseliani, a true master of acoustic side-scenes. Ossip Mandelstam, a poet from St. Petersburg who visited Tbilisi some forty years before the films came out, characterized the sounds of Tbilisi with the *sazandari*, a kind of chamber orchestra of the East. If we are tempted to accuse Mandelstam of orientalizing Tbilisi, we would do well to remind ourselves of Ioseb Grishashvili's *Literary Bohemia of Old Tbilisi* (1927). Here, we learn from him that the sound of Tbilisi at the dawn of the 20th century was one of acoustic difference – *polyphonic*, to be more precise.

Tbilisi was indeed a certain polyphonic cosmopolis, at least on the Caucasian scale. The city remained open to the foreign at the same time making this foreign its own. In the Tbilisi of the 19th century, an Imeretian from western Georgia looked more foreign than an Armenian or a Turk. Those doubting my words are advised again to consult the classics, this time *My Adventure* (1894–1908) by Akaki Tsereteli. There is a story in the book about the culture shock the author's father faced when he witnessed the manners and apparel of a serf who had returned from Tbilisi. The feasts á la Tbilisi were not known among Imeretians. They ate and drank in different ways. Even the distinction between the spoken languages was once so large that it made Prince Grigol Orbeliani lament how unintelligible the prose of western Georgian author Sergei Meskhi were: »Meskhi writes and, alas, leaves the readers all aghast«[4].

In the 1920s, Tbilisi was a site of encounter between local poets and a large group of artists, writers, poets, and actors who had fled the Russian Revolution. During this period, Tbilisi was transformed into a real cosmopolis and one of the capitals of the avant-garde. The majority of *Tsisperkantselebi* (the Blue Horns, the most important group of mostly symbolist poets and writers in 20th-century Georgia originally founded in 1915 Kutaisi) were, by 1918, Tbilisians by choice if not by origin. It was they, in particular Titsian Tabidze, who devised a formula that explained the essence of the city: »The rose of Hafiz in *la vase brise* of Prudhomme.«

Tbilisi, as a cosmopolis, came to an end in 1921. Isn't it tragic that Georgian communists, such as Philipe Makharadze and Budu Mdivani, would prove much harsher nationalists than any political party that had claimed nationalism? The Georgian Bolsheviks became nationalist in the narrowest, ethnic, provincial sense, which defined Georgian Nationalism in the Soviet period and continues to define, to a certain extent, political

3 აკა მორჩილაძე, გადაფრენა მადათოვზე და უკან, (თბილისი 1998)
4 გრიგოლ ორბელიანი, თხზულებათა სრული კრებული, რედ. აკაკი გაწერელია და ჯუმბერ ჭუმბურიძე, (თბილისი 1959)

orientations even today. Thus began the age of ethnicization and provincialization of Tbilisi and Georgia more generally. Soviet urbanization policy made sure this process became irreversible. The artificial transformation of Tbilisi into a million-city (a Soviet term for a city with a population of a million or more), for the seemingly innocuous cause of obtaining budgetary preference, completely changed the cityscape and affected the ethnic balance. Furthermore, in the chaos of the 1990s, the former cosmopolis started to suffer the outflow of non-Georgian ethnic groups.

A cosmopolis is a risky place or, more precisely, a place of risk. Without the bold daring to part with his own identity, a human, as well as a city, is doomed to repeat the same experience in terms of consciousness and to remain provincial in terms of its spatiality. The risk of giving up identity, the risk of change with an uncertain outcome, is a precondition of freedom. A cosmopolis creates spaces for human beings to transcend their own limits, to fulfill or realize themselves, albeit without guaranteeing the success of this undertaking. On the other hand, when a city closes its doors and imposes a certain order or certain identity on its citizens (national, ethnic or whatever), it ceases to be a city with ambitions to accumulate the whole world or the whole cosmos and turns into a provincial town. This is what happened to Tbilisi during Soviet times. Let's hope it will open itself once more.

My Street

Matthias Klingenberg

I've lived on Tsagareli Street in the Saburtalo district of Tbilisi since February 2012. It was named after the internationally unknown Georgian geologist Archil Tsagareli in 1991. Before then, it was called Kronstadt Street, in memory of the fortress town in northern Russia that played a vital role in the seaward defense of Leningrad against the Germans in World War II.

None of that figured into considerations about my choice of residence. It was much more that at first sight I very much liked the street and the Soviet-era house on it. Not only that, the brick house with its beige transom windows, its huge terrace, and a little garden with figs, grapes, and beautiful rose bushes, reminded me of my house in distant Tashkent where I lived and worked many years ago. My feelings of nostalgia probably also had something to do with the time I spent with the mother of my daughter in Tashkent – a perfect family beneath a starry Asian sky … or something like that. In those days, at the beginning of 2012, Tsagareli was still a dreamy, little-used side street of small houses and aromatic gardens. It was the precise image of the Caucasus that a Western expat would paint for himself.

But half a year after I moved here, the picture began to change. It started with an ancient, rusty, oily GAZ lorry. The Soviet flatbed truck, with its elongated, old-style nose, was standing on the road with its loading-bed facing the gate to my neighbor's house, blocking traffic and provoking a hysterical symphony of car horns that only then made me aware of the fact that men in black, fake leather jackets, stained jeans, and cheap mirrored sunglasses were clearing out my neighbors' belongings from the house and onto the truck. The fact that this was no ordinary move quickly became clear as I came closer and noticed that they had torn the windows from their frames and thrown them onto the pavement, where the panes were already lying smashed.

I watched for a while, still vaguely hoping that they were just planning to modernize the beautiful brick house with its curlicue cast-iron balconies. But it soon became clear that this hope had no foundation. That same evening the men returned with their Soviet lorry, this time to dismantle the roof with an ear-shattering racket. The roof was carefully deconstructed, beam-by-beam, nails torn out and thrown on the flatbed, and the wood set aside to be recycled. The next day they removed all the window frames and doors, and on the third day they began to dismantle the entire house, stone by stone, and load it onto the old GAZ truck still parked on the street. Why didn't they just order an excavator and raze the building to the ground, which would have been a lot quicker? At first I thought the new owners were just trying to save money since manual labor costs next to nothing in Georgia, but then I learned that those red bricks, once freed from their old mortar, had their own considerable value. Dato, the foreman, explained this to me when I went over to him at the end of the week to find out what this was all about. Apparently, many rich Georgians will pay up to one lari apiece for these stones and use them in their nostalgic country houses in the mountains outside of Tbilisi.

Here, then, is a textbook symptom of the new Tbilisi: classic old brick city houses torn down without a second thought and their stones reused to build nostalgic, red-brick, bourgeois villas outside of town.

Opposite me on Tsagareli Street, in a less beautiful grey-plastered house, lived Zurab with his mother. On weekdays when I came home from work, she would sit there and stare at me – her arms folded on a grubby cushion. But she never once greeted me, or indeed moved. Not that I was complaining – I could live without her affection. Unfortunately, her son Zurab, a man in his mid-thirties, showed an inordinate interest in me. He rang my bell soon after I moved in; but rather than welcoming his new neighbor with the traditional bread and salt, he wanted to borrow money. He had a number of problems – his black Mercedes was losing oil, a friend owed him money and should have paid him back ages ago, etc., etc. Long story short – could I lend him 20 lari? I didn't hesitate much, but handed him a twenty and accepted his promise that I'd be seeing the note again the following Monday. Of course I didn't imagine for a second that I would ever get the money back. But apparently I was doing Zurab a disservice. Next Monday there he was standing punctually at my door again, as agreed – this time unshaven and with a rich smell of alcohol on his breath. He thanked me and returned the cash.

This happened a few more times over the next year – sometimes 20, sometimes 10, sometimes even 50 lari – but I always got the money back on time so that little by little we became good neighbors. Our conversations gradually lengthened. At some point I asked what he thought about the drastic changes in our neighborhood – by this time almost half of the old houses had been demolished and replaced by precarious, half-finished new constructions. He smiled and said that he too would soon be the owner of a new nine to twelve-story block; that they were

The GAZ flatbed truck bringing materials to the construction site on Tsagareli Street, with typical rendering of new flats taking their place against a backdrop of the same.

planning to tear down his ugly house, and that it was just a matter of time before he himself would be selling luxury apartments. I looked at Zurab rather skeptically, considered his broken, gappy teeth, thought of his old wheezing Mercedes from the early 80s, and smiled back. »Yes, Zurab, yes – just a matter of time. Have a good night!« After I'd locked the heavy steel door (my house had previously been inhabited by security-conscious employees of the American embassy) I poured myself a glass of Saperavi and laughed heartily at Zurab's foolish and ridiculously inflated opinion of himself.

But that laughter was soon caught in my throat. Less than a month later a filthy old lorry turned up on the street and men with cheap sunglasses loaded furniture and clothes wrapped in bed sheets onto it, and the following day began to destroy the roof of the ugly building opposite mine. The entire demolition and subsequent construction work was overseen by Zurab, who was sure to throw me an occasional sardonic glance as he spat cigarette stubs onto the asphalt and reached self-importantly for his smartphone. He rarely missed a chance to scratch contentedly at his belly.

As for the so-called ›new construction‹, at some point, after about six months had gone by, I found myself walking past a newly completed shell. Dato was sitting in front of the concrete skeleton eating grapes. I couldn't help but notice that the shell was standing very crookedly on its foundation. So crookedly that even I, a passerby who had merely glanced over, could tell. I called to Dato and told him, in a playfully presumptuous undertone, that his house was wonky and a blind man on crutches could see it. Dato chewed the grape he had just put in his mouth, swallowed it with relish, and then said curtly: »It's straight enough for us Georgians.« I couldn't think of a quick answer to this so responded instead with a brief Russian *ponyatno*, or »I understand«, and went on my way.

The problem with these new buildings isn't just that they are a deeply unpleasant mish-mash of styles, but that their erection inevitably involves horrific noises, smells, and amateurish execution. For example, to this day it's still not clear to me what you gain by pouring concrete at night, apart from the fact that the noise is a lot more annoying. I don't understand how the process can be sensibly managed without light. I mean, you can't actually see where the concrete is being poured. And so it came as no surprise when gallons of cement flowed into the neighboring garden, onto the roof, and dripped onto the garden furniture during the construction of the new block, as no one noticed it flowing over the edges of its formwork. I'd rather not go into how I was without water for a month in the spring of 2014 after the builders decided to turn off my water supply when it was minus 10 degrees outside, whereupon my pipes froze and burst. What I would like to talk about is what happens to these buildings, or rather about the flats inside them, because that seems more important. For up until now, precisely nothing has actually happened – almost all the flats that have been declared habitable are still empty. In fact, only one flat per building is inhabited, where the former owner of the beautiful old brick house lives – that posh new apartment was part of his deal with the constructors. Could it be that locals have noticed that these houses are more like Brazilian favelas than something fit for the new pro-European Georgia and that this is why so few buyers have turned up?

While that seemed logical to me it somehow didn't square with my image of Georgia. So I asked Dato, who informed me that the apartments had been sold to investors in bunches, or even entire blocks, who then traded them on the international property market. So that was the big business transpiring on my street, of which, unfortunately, my neighbor and his brigade did not get much of a share. With this, many things about Georgia were becoming clearer to me.

Historic Saburtalo neighborhood fabric in the foreground, set against the towering new buildings that take its place. Both coexisting in this fragile moment.

Neighborhoods
Kakha Tolordava

Gldani If you are predisposed to disdain typically Soviet housing districts, then roaming around any *microraion* (sleeping quarter or microdistrict) on the outskirts of Tbilisi is a complete waste of time. But this is true only for those who prejudge the area. Incredulous of any good to come of sleeping quarters in general, these people are apt to reach the hasty conclusion that it is a place of complete existential and architectural chaos. But the day I spent in Gldani served as further proof that wandering through the blocks can be an extraordinarily productive experience when your mind is in a creative mode.

I suspect those who originally planned Gldani were experiencing that very creativity when they were designing – as it is a marvelously conceived and arranged district. I fear its planners just did not have the time to complete their creature, and that is why Gldani remains so underdone. Its final finish was saved for the simple passage of time and the accompanying storm of change.

Gldani is composed of three parts and all three have tremendous potential for further development. A central core runs through the length of the district and offers significant space for experimentation with new ideas. I usually refer to this strip as the »show-off part« as it has the pontential to be an important part of cultural life in Gldani. Each time I find myself here, I feel that the primary purpose of any visit is to imagine what can be done in this space tomorrow, rather than concentrating on what it is today. The same applies to the actual Soviet-faced sleeping quarters. I find it the only place in the city where repainting the facade might not be a bad idea after all.

Private initiatives of local inhabitants – enlarging flats by building-out balconies, fencing common yards for garages, and other uncontrollable practices – have successfully defaced a district that has, in fact, always invited defacement.

The Gldani of today is a space open for experimentation. This is the primary quality it has retained from its conception. And this is why it is so regrettable that its bad reputation does not invite people to spark new ideas for its transformation or to advocate for more municipal services. Basically, this is the tragedy of all the sleeping quarters: the wake-up-buy-eat-consume-have-fun-at-the-amusement-park-go-to-bed-wake-up attitude. Gldani is a bit more fortunate in this sense, as there is a theater here and the district even had its own nightclub. What is essential is that Gldani (or Varketili Didi-Dighomi, or any other *microraion* for that matter) requires much more attention than it has enjoyed to date. With a sound approach and decent advocacy, Gldani could easily be transformed into a very decent neighborhood. If I could, I would bring school children on trips to the outskirts and share with them what has been done, what is being done, and what can be done in such areas.

Avlabari Each street in Avlabari invites you to stay longer than anywhere else. Each courtyard welcomes you to take a look inside. You want to know the locals. You want to be a local. The November sun is at my back, throwing my shadow in front of me. I've been walking along Avlabari Street for about twenty minutes. The words I can hear are mainly spoken in Armenian and Russian. The boys have a heavy look; the girls wear bright colors and laugh more than elsewhere. »Enriko galisa?« asks a ten-year-old boy with a school bag. I stop and look around to help him find his friend Enriko. I can't see him. The boys reconnect and continue on their way. As I look at them, I remember I've never taken a walk here in winter's snow. Nor have I brought my child here. Why? I don't know.

A blue car on the corner of the street belts out a Russian song at full volume. But if you just take a couple of more turns, you'll find yourself in complete silence. It is like that wherever you go in this neighborhood. One moment you are surrounded by the sounds of the city and next you can only hear your feet scratching the leaves on the tarmac. In a few seconds, even the sound is gone and a narrow side street leaves you in solitude with your footsteps and heartbeat. None of these streets leave you alone without a gift. When you step back into the noisy city, you will carry with you the memories of what you saw: a couple of brick houses – slightly damaged, with chaotically beautiful courtyards, sometimes with a cypress tree – the walls painted here with a portrait of Schwarzenegger and there with stencils made of Lowenbrau cans protruding from a window.

I love the street maze here, but I'm not really sure if the locals share my viewpoint. Laundry lines start and end in different courtyards. Water heaters are installed on trees outside the houses. And power lines compose an intricate labyrinth. Surely this can't be the result of an easy life, and one is amazed at how the locals manage to park their cars in these narrow, inaccessible streets. Do they use helicopters to lower them at night and use the same device in the morning to take them out? Yet when you meet a local they are more likely smiling than frowning. Moreover, it is while walking here that you feel how much the heart of the city is in fact centered here. Tbilisi is sprawling this way and that – very slowly but steadily. Numerous new construction sites speak of this fact. But thinking about the sprawling outskirts of town makes you wonder how it is possible that the uniquely chaotic and damaged beauty of this place is retained.

A woman disrupts my thoughts. »Are you from the gas company?« she asks in Georgian. »No, I'm not, madam!« »Is it about divergence of the railway then?« I hastily hide my notebook and pen and walk on. In a few minutes I find myself following a funeral procession – it is impossible to pass. Then I'm sipping coffee with some good people, right in the street, standing, talking about politics. A woman invites me to taste her fruit; another gives me a freshly baked potato pie. »Vot vi, Vakintsi, dumaete, chto zdes nam legko, no« (You, from Vake, you think the life's easy here, but …). A while later I'm playing football in a stunningly beautiful street whose name I've failed to take down. No worries, I can find it again later. Then I get extremely exhausted and go home. As I sup, I browse the map of Tbilisi and think of another locale for another walk.

»Oh, I prefer Bvlgari,« a woman says next to me. It's morning. I'm sitting at Turtle Lake writing this. All of this reminds me of the burned smell of leaves while walking in the streets of Avlabari.

Avchala First I follow scars left by the former tramway. Then I go right, cross the street, and get to a rural-looking area via blocks of repetitive flats lining the main road. It's a maze of streets and alleys. The warm breeze brings a phantom aroma of the sea – from where I do not know.

71

Then it smells of railway parts and only after that – of cow dung. Each of these three smells suggests its own aspect of the area.

The scent of the sea is followed by a pink house with an arcade over the balcony and vine-covered façade. The railway smell is accompanied first by a girl at the bus stop, in red nail polish, holding a psalm book, and then by a boy with his lips red from the pomegranate he's clutching. The dung is the smell of the maze of houses and orchards where I'm walking now. There's a ruined arcade at the beginning of the slope. There's no one nearby. At least, I think there's no one, until I hear someone shouting: »There's no way further there!« Only then I notice a man with his head on the white, stone wall. The man smiles, and that's how I know I'm not just talking to a head. It's going to rain.

While in Zemo Avchala, if you pay proper attention, and if the outskirts don't automatically depress you, you'll easily notice both the rhythm and the mood are different. This must be due in part to the open space, as well as the cool northern breeze that carries the smell of the forest. Before I got here, I took some photos of a huge flock of sheep, shepherds, a transparent police building, and even a ruined car abandoned in the middle of the street. »Is everything alright?« some passerby asks me. »Yes, it's fine,« I assure him. »Good« he answers, turns to the cross erected on the mountain, and crosses himself. Two young women and the gentleman standing in front of us join him in this. Before I continue on my way, I throw a surprised look at the *marchrutka* with big letters reading »Saburtalo« on its side. I can feel the distance overpowering me.

Now I turn to the left, to the Mtkvari, to the area that was called *avi chala* (evil grove) in the past. I've been wandering in the area for nearly two hours, but I still find the energy of this evil part the best. The only thing that I'm concerned about is that I'm obviously perceived as a foreigner by the locals, even though I'm not giving them any reason to do so. I'm basically an ordinarily dressed, middle-aged, bald man, only drawing his camera when needed. Yet I feel their looks when they pass. I don't like this, but what can I do? Then it dawns on me – can you see anyone else taking a photo of the trousers hanging to dry on the fence?

I take Bichvinta Street to get to the historical fortress inside Vakhtang Lomishvili's yard. It's one of the twelve fortresses remaining from the 18th century. It is really beautiful, but today I can only look at it from a distance. There's a wedding ceremony in the church and the place is packed with people and cars. The whole scene leads me to give up any attempt to look at the fortress properly, so I wait for the emergence of the bride and groom from the church along with many smartly dressed young men. The air smells of the river here.

A sickly looking dog follows me at the empty railway platform – ten, fifteen steps, no less. I am marching towards the city, not knowing where exactly the dirt road will take me. I stop a woman: »Good afternoon. Where will this road take me?« She eyes me with suspicion, then the dog too, and asks: »Are you an American?«

2 Building Soviet Tbilisi

a

b

c

d

e

f

g

h

k

l

Building Soviet Tbilisi

The nature of Georgian modern architecture is, like that of so many former Soviet Republics, inseparable from the economic and social vision that lies at its base. If the central pillar of Soviet state-building was its planned economy, then of course we can expect to find a planned landscape as its corollary. Spaces for living, spaces for working, spaces for leisure, and spaces for health, were all specific nodes within a crystalline landscape that had this centralized economy at its core. But like so many other regionally specific articulations of these centralizing tendencies, much of the Soviet-era architecture of Tbilisi is simultaneously a material counter to any dream of pure systematization. In it we can see tensions that can be located at the heart the Soviet diagram: tensions between the one and the many, between specificity and generality, between standardization and authorship, and between bureaucracy and beauty. In the archive shared here, part of the National Archives of Georgia, we can see these tensions played out in the combined singularity and repetition of building form, landscape articulation, and programmatic types.

a   Mukhiani district which was master-planned in the State Designing Institute *Tbilqalaqproeqti* Department of City Planning (headed by Givi Shavdia). Aerial picture from 1981.

b   Aerial picture of the Ministry of Highway Construction from 1987, designed by Giorgi Chakhava and Zurab Jalagania in 1975.

c   Wedding Palace on an aerial picture from 1987, built by Victor Jorbenadze and Structural Engineer Givi Pitskhelauri in 1984.

d   Aquatic sports complex Laguna Vere on an aerial picture from 1988 constructed by Shota Kavlashvili, Ramaz Kiknadze and Guram Abuladze with monumental mosaics by Koka Ignatov.

e   Newly built Varketili district on an aerial picture from 1987.

f   Hotel *Iveria* built by architect Otar Kalandarishvili (with participation of Ia Tskhomelidze) in 1967. Aerial picture from 1988.

g   Aeroflot ticket office *Aerovogzal* at Sandukeli-Road built by Otar Kalandarishvil on an aerial picture from 1972.

h   Palace of Chess and Alpinism (Lado Aleksi Meskhishvili and Germane Gudushauri), Philharmonic Hall Rotunda by Ivane Chkhenkeli and prestigious apartment house (Shota Kavlashvili and Ramaz Kiknadze) on an aerial picture from 1987.

i   Road intersection and Bridge in Mtskheta, planned and realized by the Ministry of Highway Construction on an aerial picture from 1987.

j   The former Post Office building was designed by Lado Aleksi-Meskhishvili and Teimuraz Mikashavidze. Aerial picture from 1979.

k   Memorial for Georgian poet Nikoloz Baratashvili by architect Shota Kavlashvili on an aerial picture from 1981.

l   All Republican Hospital by architect Mikheil Shavishvil on an aerial picture from 1988.

Testing Grounds
Jesse Vogler

On the far north end of Tbilisi, on a low-lying bend in the Mtkvari River, is a collection of large houses reminiscent of a North American suburban development. Aggressively walled parcels mask exuberant stand-alone houses – some in a modified Spanish Renaissance style, some in a disproportionate classical language, and most with an awkward modernist cast – and all with a defiant singularity that stands in marked contrast with every other housing type in the city. Here, in the Digomi Dachas, we have the sclerotic privacy of an American form of suburbanism cast into the space of a 5th-century city. Here, we have Tbilisi's preeminent enclave urbanism.

A glance at an aerial view will show a street grid set at neat 45-degree angles to north, and equally canted from the predominant road network that surrounds it. Large rectangular blocks, delineated by rows of trees, inscribe a gridded street form seemingly immanent to an unseen, abstract topography. Houses and lots begin to fill in the blocks in an inexorable consummation of the logic of private property. The presence of the Mtkvari River to the east is an apparent afterthought to a street pattern that is seemingly resolute in ignoring its geographic context.

You might be tempted to read this enclave, as I first was, as a particularly Georgian translation of an American suburban form – inefficient, geometrically overdetermined, and socially evacuated. But in this we are only partially correct. For the very street pattern that determines orienta-

Aerial picture of Tbilisi *meurneoba* as it looked in 2006.

tion, parcel frontage, and the neighborhood fabric is in fact a vestige from an earlier spatial moment. Digomi Dachas are in fact built within the former field patterns, turnrows, and agricultural logics of Tbilisi's experimental state farm. The result is a disorienting, hermit-crab situation – a new, post-1990 privatized enclave built within the carapace of collectivized agricultural land.

The Tbilisi test farm was part of the large-scale Soviet agricultural planning of the mid-20th century. With the socialization of land that followed from the Bolshevik land decree of 1917, it fell on the newly land-rich state to define the best systems for agricultural production. State farms fell into two broad categories: *kolhoz*, collective farms; and *sovkhoze* (*meurneoba* in Georgian), state-owned farms. The former can perhaps best be imagined as a new federation of already-existing farmsteads that were brought under a new centralized control of a soviet. The latter, however, were usually located in places where farming practices were either highly inefficient or simply non-existent – and became the highly centralized, large-scale, de novo farms of the Soviet imaginary. Such is the case with the Tbilisi test farm.

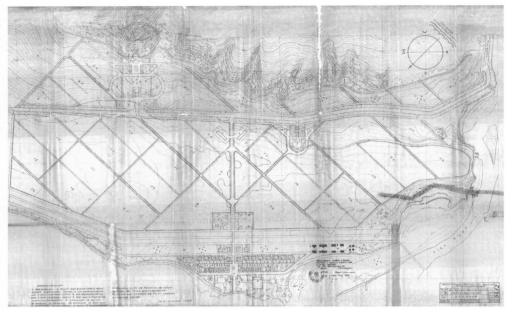

Plan of the Tbilisi *meurneoba*, showing fields, roads, and shelterbelts set at a 45-degree angle to north, adjusted to block prevailing winds. Note compass rose and the callout for primary wind direction.

The Tbilisi *meurneoba*, originally laid out in 1947, was sited on the far north edge of the city on a wide, fertile bend in the river. Occupying a terrace between the floodplain and the hillside, this territory was home to a diverse set of crop and fruit experiments. Here agronomists tested new grape varieties, experimented with fruit tree hardiness, developed new tomato hybrids, and set to work on a range of productive landscape tests.

Associated with this test farm was a small village wedged between the test plots and the floodplain edge. As with so much rural planning at this time, this settlement was seen as a self-contained village – with housing, schools, civic buildings, and canteen taking their places alongside the production infrastructures for the farm. To this day, the original village can be found if you follow the old roads toward the river, beyond the walls of the new houses, where the classical proportions of Stalinist-era housing and public buildings are nestled beneath the heavy canopy of evergreen trees.

The street orientation of the *meurneoba*, with its strong geometric figure incised on the planar ground, appears at first glance to be the stuff of pure modernist hubris. But far from a geometrical deviation from the environment, it is in fact a highly responsive pivot within it – with one axis aligned with the direction of the predominant winds. The compass rose on the upper right of the plan makes apparent the climatic response that the designers intended. This aeolian axis sets the rigid geometry of the grid on its edge, resulting in the sharp disorientation of the territory.

These wind-oriented streets and fields in turn offered a test bed for one of the Soviets' most prolific landscape type – the shelterbelt. Long before the epic articulation of Stalin's Great Plan for the Transformation of Nature, Soviet scientists had been at work testing the efficacy of particular tree species and their distribution in keeping winds and associated dust at bay. Part of a larger national imperative aimed at wholesale environmental transformation, the shelterbelt was the landscape technology of choice for fighting the threats posed by the internal eastern front – desertification and dust.

Tbilisi's test farm was associated with the large National Agricultural University that sat on the topographic rise to the west. As one in a network of agricultural schools across the former Union, the AgriUni was Georgia's primary vehicle through which new practices, technologies, and products were tested and disseminated across the Republic. It was, in many ways, one of the purest articulations of both central economic planning and centralized land-use practices in the vast Soviet diagram. Ironic, then, that this would come to be the poster child in post-collapse land privatization.

For it is here, in the former state farms and test plots, that one of Tbilisi's most aggressive experiments in land privatization and single-family housing can be found. In the years following the collapse of the Soviet Union, and with the nascent promise of a looming land boom, the rector of the university moved to liquidate the university's landholdings in one of the largest privatization binges in the city. Here the large test plots and experimental fields were seen, through the newly valued logic of real estate, as a particularly convenient tract for privatizing. The fields were parceled up and given addresses, and the turnrows paved and given street names. What remained of the original meurneoba village center drifted toward a new periphery.

In place of the fields and shelterbelts have risen the walls and gates of the intensely fortified development we know today. To build in Digomi is to announce that one has arrived. As a friend quipped: »King Erekle didn't even have a house like this!« It is all the former situation of the Soviet period was not: private, singular, and chosen. The houses of this area are barely visible above the three to four- meter walls that rise along the newly significant property line at the street edge. The resulting landscape is one of abstract isolation, with the large, closed gates both showing and saying (communicating and performing, announcing and showing) their shut-ness.

Yet what we can see of these houses speaks to an emerging value system clearly at odds with the gray standardization of the typical soviet housing model. Ornate cornices terminate in precarious parapets; bronzed spandrel glass resolves itself in orange and yellow stuccos. It is, to be sure, an exuberant expression of a new moment. Defiantly distinct and architecturally inscrutable, these homes nonetheless express, as clearly as anything else in the landscape, a new ideology of speculation and individuation. And like the ideologically motivated state farms and collective housing that came before them, this landscape will go on believing for us long after the condition of its emergence has gone.

Typical Dighomi Dachas. Promiscuous in their privacy.

Fruit tree test plot in the Tbilisi meurneoba. Individual trees are wrapped in cloches to protect from frost.

Realizing Utopias
Levan Kalandarishvili

Street Houses named Desire   The Housing for Tramway Workers, built in 1926 in Tbilisi, is the last witness of a Soviet, utopian, social-architectural impulse that sustains its function in the present. This housing complex was the first example of integrated social housing in Tbilisi, where blocks of standardized apartments were merged with a full set of community services. The block types are composed of standardized housing plans of 2, 3, and 4 rooms, in addition to one-room, dormitory type blocks. All of these housing types are then provided with a full suite of community services including bath, laundry, shop, library, dining hall for 100 people, and a doctor's office. Designed by well-known Tbilisi architect David Chisliev, the complex is also remarkable for its transitional façade, which reflects the artistic aspirations between national and international forms.

At the time Chisliev was commissioned for the execution of the project he was the deputy director of Tiflis Committee of State Buildings. The housing complex was designed on a two-hectare site on the edge of the former German colonies of Neue Tiflis and Alexandersdorf, immediately adjacent to the famous Mushtaid Gardens. The initial design consisted of twelve rectangular blocks in two rows, but in the end only eight buildings were erected and according to a different plan. And in the first decade of the 21st century, the authors of the Rose Revolution altered the buildings to show their own vision of a post-Soviet »utopia,« giving us the chance to see the perception of Thomas More's renaissance dream-island articulated by a different type of statesman.

So let's follow the history of this complex through time: as it was proposed by the architect Chisliev; as it was built by the Tbilisi City Council of Soviets; as it was altered according to young politicians' taste in early 21st century; and as it looks today.

What was the architect's original vision for the social space of the complex? Chisliev's design included a bathhouse, laundry, workers cooperative, dining hall, and other public amenities that were originally planned to be located in the northeast part of the site. Below is a free interpretation of the architect's goals for the building, as given in an article published in the fifth edition of the *Official Journal of Tiflis City Council of Workers, Peasants and Red Army Soldiers*, from May 1926:

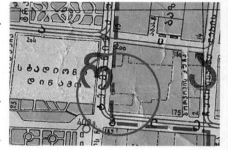

Site plan of the Housing for Tramway Workers in 1934 and in 2016.

1   Baths are to be located in a well-lit basement level, with hot water provided 24 hours a day. The architect notes that there should be separate sections for men and women, with an ante-room for hanging outer garments, a middle room with armchairs and wardrobes for under clothes, and a washing room with tubs and other equipment. Considering the proposed capacity of the bath – 480 people each twelve-hour cycle – each of the 1,500 inhabitants would have access twice a week.

2   Laundries are to be located in the same building with hot water provided by the same source, and will be able to wash 60 poods (over one ton) per day.

3   Four *mushcoop* (workers cooperatives) shops are to be located in each building, with two per side at the parade entrance of the singles' block on Plekhanov Street – half for groceries, half for manufactured goods, etc. Shops are to have storage in the basement.

The same block will accommodate the library, reading room, and Lenin's corner.

4   A fully-equipped dining hall (food and wood storage, freezer, dish-washer etc) with a veranda is to be located in the singles' block on Plekhanov Street.

5   Administration, doctor's office, kindergarten, and children's nursery are to be located in the same block.

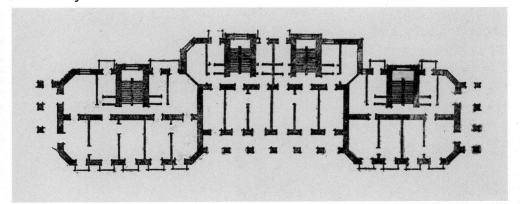

Typical floor plan for families' block with 3-4 + 2-2-2 + 3-4 room distribution on the Tsabadze street (former Telman, original Mushtaidi).

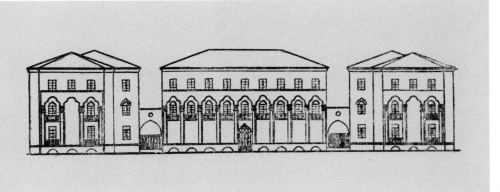

Façade from Agmashenebeli Prospekt (former Plexanov, original Mikhael's Prospekt).

Special attention was to be paid to the water supply, canalization, and waste boxes, with yards and sidewalks to be paved with trees planted alongside them. Additionally, fire hydrants were to be installed in the appropriate places and a central heating system, running on steam, was to be provided from two boilers located in the basement of the singles' block.

Despite the fact that the complex, as built, was not serviced by all of these promised amenities, the vitality of these apartment blocks is really astonishing. We believe that this is an important typological reference for application in contemporary urban situations, to make our city healthier and to create a better environment for the neighborhood.

I do not have access to all the documents regarding contemporary rehabilitation and construction of this quarter; however, I have personally known a lot of people including classmates, their parents, and neighbors who have lived in these houses from the very beginning and who remain attached to this place. If there were a chance, it would be interesting to talk with other inhabitants who transformed their apartments into their own »utopias,« with those who justified the logic of renovation, and those who approved it in the city's architectural service. The challenge of rehabilitation, adaptation, and revitalization of traditional Tbilisi neighborhoods in an appropriate way is of utmost importance, and it depends on the inclusive approach of many parties.

When Dreams Don't Come True   In the early 1930s Georgian architecture changed direction toward the so-called »Stalinist Empire« style, and until the mid-1950s it had little in common with avant-garde, constructivist, or utopian approaches. And while modernist tendencies of the late 1950s and early 1960s gave more flexibility to creative architects, this was proscribed by certain limits and took place within the frame of building codes tailored to the needs of a mass-construction industry rather than the creativity of a single architect.

One of the most consistent architects, and one who never betrayed his constructivist architectural taste, was the modernist architect Joseph Zaalishvili (1905–1985). He won a competition for the reconstruction of Rustaveli Square with a proposal centered around transforming Rustaveli Avenue (Tbilisi's main street) into a pedestrian road – but his

Model for a reconstruction of Rustaveli Square from 1965 by a group of architects under Ioseb Zaalishvili.

ideas were not ultimately shared and another project was chosen for construction. His most successful architectural ideas were realized in the many recreational buildings he designed and had built across Georgia.

His rival during the Rustaveli contest, architect Otar Kalandarishvili, received the commission ten years after the first competition; but time has shown that his approach was not built around a long-term urban perspective and was inconsistent with local spatial organizations and aesthetic values.

The design for the Monument of the Stalinist Purges, a collaboration between architect Rezo Beridze and sculptor Juna Mikatadze, is another example of an unrealized project of the early 1980s. Despite many discussions, agreements, and promises, the vision for the memorial, like its authors, died. This project was particularly interesting for its new interpretation of Georgian religious architectural motifs in a modern form.

In this same period, Otar Kalandarishvili decided to diversify the gray, outer neighborhoods by rethinking traditional forms of tower construction found in the mountain regions of Georgia. A series of three, typical sixteen-story blocks, built on the steep slopes of the Nutsubidze plateau, were connected with a network of metal bridges facilitating inhabitants' access on different levels – constructing a street in the sky.

Architects Tevzadze, Morbedadze, and Kandelaki designed a project for a multimodal building at an important junction of bus, rail and subway transport, which facilitated passenger movement to and from the airport. The resulting project is a transportation hub in the form of a UFO. Architect Avtandil Sumbulashvili, in his unrealized project for the Didi-Digomi neighborhood, also tried to connect two microdistricts by coordinating open public spaces between them.

The 1989 competition for the erection of the Trinity Cathedral Church was also significant in that it marked the transformation of typical Soviet architects into »believers.« The conservative character of the competition's program reflected the unpreparedness of the architectural community to meet this new challenge. The result is disappointing. The main cathedral of Tbilisi, with its out-sized repetition of Georgian church architecture, dominates the city like a massive decoration for a historical film. This underscores an architectural irony where the construction of churches is transformed into a profitable business. So, instead of rehabilitating real heritage sites we are witnessing the erection of new, concrete churches that mechanically repeat historical ornamentation from the past.

If we look over the past twenty-five years of Georgian architecture, the evidence is rather pessimistic: little desire to understand heritage (even of the 20th-century sort), pseudo-historical approaches, and a singular orientation toward private investment. Certainly the »skyscraperization« of the city as well as the »rurbanization« of buildings is an interesting socio-cultural phenomenon for research – but it has nothing to do with a healthy recovery of the urban environment.

Rapid urban development, as well as the latest innovations in the construction industry, gives us a lot of material for rethinking how and where contemporary architecture should be headed; however, everyday life shows that the space for real architectural utopias is becoming smaller and smaller, and is confined to the work of conceptual art rather than into feasible architectural plans. I think this is the main challenge and aspiration that both old and young architects should unite around and fight for.

Up in the Air: Traces of Aerial Connectivity

Suzanne Harris-Brandts
and David Gogishvili

The panoramic view of Rose Revolution Square from Alexander Griboyedov Street would be perfect, were it not for the unsightly presence of a large, abandoned concrete column still extending metal rebar and wrapped in wooden construction formwork. Closer attention reveals a larger unsightly construction site at the base: a rugged enclosure of sheet-metal hoarding stretches around the area and an ever-accumulating garbage heap forms within its abandoned confines. This is the rejected location of the new gondola line intended to connect Rose Revolution Square to Mtatsminda Park, proposed by the Georgian government in 2012.[1] The lofty project was supposed to bring fresh life into the square, and as such, was in keeping with the fervor of urban transformation underway across Tbilisi after the 2003 Rose Revolution. Here specifically, at the former political meeting point of Republic Square (renamed Rose Revolution Square in 2005), a new gondola connection promised to update the area and work towards luring additional visitors. The project was in line with other nearby architectural transformations underway since Georgia's independence, including the refurbishment of the famous Iveria Hotel and the demolition of the Soviet-era monument ›Andropov's Ears‹/Rustaveli Arches at the square's northern edge. Despite this pace of change, the gondola project was ultimately suspended in November 2014 due to strong local opposition.[2] Owners of the Iveria Hotel felt that the project raised security concerns for their property and local residents feared the design would be out of context with its historic surroundings.[3]

This article traces the history of Tbilisi's cable car transportation network and examines its contemporary transformations during a period of politico-economic volatility: when Georgia went from a republic within the Soviet Union to an independent capitalist nation. The Soviets produced seven cable car lines between 1957 and 1986 that were distributed relatively evenly across Tbilisi, from as far southeast as Samgori to as far northwest as Didube. Others were planned or already under construction at the time of the Soviet Union's collapse in 1991.[4] These lines served two primary functions: connecting urban areas up to natural recreation spaces in the city's mountainous outskirts, and extensions of the public transit network. Following the collapse of the Soviet Union, these lines were decommissioned, but today new urban regeneration initiatives are again considering their feasibility.[5] Across Tbilisi signs of revitalized aerial cable transit corridors can now be seen. They exist alongside traces of the city's former abandoned cable car legacy, the relics of which have also undergone ad-hoc spatial appropriation and integration with their surroundings.

From Crucial Infrastructure to Soviet Ruin   Less than one hundred meters west of the half-finished column at Revolution Square is another frozen-in-time, hoarded-up site tucked inside the courtyard of the National Academy of Science building. This is the original, cultural heritage listed, lower-station cable car building that connected Rustaveli up to Mtatsminda Park beginning in 1957. It is here that the history of Georgia's aerial cable car infrastructure officially began, following the earlier success of the railed 1905 funicular cable car line connecting city residents to Mtatsminda

1   თბილისში ახალი საბაგირო გაიხსნა. *Tabula*, accessed 2016, www.tabula.ge/ge/story/60283-tbilisshi-axali-sabagiro-gaixsna
2   Gurgenidze, T. and Weber, S., *Out of Place*. See this book, 205-209
3   News.ge, 2014.
4   Kverenchkiladze, R., »შიგასაქალაქო ტრანსპორტი.« In თბილისი: ეკონომიკურ-გეოგრაფიული გამოკვლევა edited by V. Jaoshvili, 251-264. Tbilisi: საბჭოთა საქართველო.

5   Tabula, 2012; City.Kvira.Ge (2016) თსუ-ს მალლივი კორპუსის ბაგებთან დამაკავშირებელი საბაგიროს რეაბილიტაცია მალე დასრულდება, accessed 2012, www.goo.gl/EKUtCU; Systra, *Tbilisi Cable Transit Master Plan: Corridors analysis and comparison.*

94

Funicular line in Tbilisi from 1977.

95

from much further up the hill at Daniel Chonkadze Street (formerly Ivan Gudovich Street).[6] The lower station cable car building (designed by the Georgian architect Konstantine Chkheidze) has an extruded oval form with dramatic archways full of glass and intricate metalwork. Following its completion in October of 1959, the cable car line brought almost half a million riders annually up to the outdoor recreational park of Mtatsminda.[7] Throughout the Soviet period, Mtatsminda was one of the most visited attractions in Georgia, facilitated by its ease of access via cable car and funicular. Yet, the physical collapse of the cable car hauling rope on June 1st, 1990 led to multiple passenger injuries and the death of fifteen people. The line was never fixed afterwards. Some twenty-five years later, like most Soviet public infrastructure, the fate of both Mtatsminda Park and its abandoned cable car line have been much publicly debated, particularly following Georgian independence. In the early 2000s, the park ceased to be a state asset and was sold to Georgian tycoon, Badri Patarkatsishvili. Its redevelopment as a recreational attraction was halted for years due to a disagreement between the owners' family and the city government, and its official operation only returned in 2009, without the reactivation of the cable car line.[8] It then took several years for the proposal of the new cable car line connecting the park to Rose Revolution Square to emerge, which is also now halted.

Since the construction of this first cable car line in 1957, Tbilisi has acquired a much larger and complex aerial transportation network – one that registers many of the broader socio-political transitions that occurred in Georgia in the decades between its time as a Soviet city and its formation into an independent nation capital. During the years of Soviet rule, Georgia's aerial transportation network served everyone from local residents to regional visitors and international tourists.[9] In contrast to the more industrial-centered cable car lines found in the Georgian cities of Kutaisi, Zestaponi, and Chiatura, Tbilisi's lines were predominantly intended to support civilian leisure activities. As such, they were in keeping with the broader Soviet ideologies about recreational infrastructure and restful vacation (*otdykh*).[10] They provided a convenient way for large numbers of people to undertake self-directed leisure by plugging into remote areas; areas otherwise inhibited by the challenging, uneven topography of the city.[11] Cable car connections also ran from Ilia Chavchavadze Avenue up to Kus Tba/Turtle Lake (built 1966) and from Nutsubidze Street up to the adjacent Lisi Lake (built 1978). In this sense, during the Soviet era the cable car network was a crucial means for expanding the natural recreation options of the city.[12] With the absence of an effective national and local government after independence, these lines experienced perpetual power outages and were slowly decommissioned. Throughout the 2000s, the Chavchavadze Avenue-Kus Tba line was able to remain intermittently functional, but it too was ultimately decommissioned between 2009–2016.[13] With the full decommissioning of the city's cable car network the number of readily-accessible outdoor leisure areas also greatly decreased.

At the time of the dissolution of the Soviet Union, a number of half-planned and partially-constructed cable car lines also existed. Some of these remained solely as »paper architecture« or as ideas in the minds of

The original Rustaveli-Mtatsminda line lower station building.

6 Elisashvili, A. როგორ შეიცვალა თბილისი. Tbilisi 2013: ბაკურ სულაკაურის გამომცემლობა.
7 Kverenchkiladze, შიგასაქალაქო ტრანსპორტი, 260.
8 Radio Tavisupleba, თბილისში მთაწმინდის პარკი გაიხსნა, accessed April 4, 2009, Retrieved from www.radiotavisupleba.ge/a/1602106.html
9 There was a total of 38 freight cable car and 30 public transit/recreation lines toward the end of the Soviet

period in 1981 (Georgian Soviet Encyclopedia, 1981, 143)
10 Koenker, D. P., *Club Red: vacation travel and the Soviet dream*. Cornell University Press, 2016.
11 Kverenchkiladze, შიგასაქალაქო ტრანსპორტი, p. 259
12 Ibid.
13 Lomidze, E., მშენებლობამ შეიძლება კუს ტბის საბაგირო შეიწიროს. Kviris Palitra, accessed July 28, 2014, www.kvirispalitra.ge/deda-

architects and planners, but two came very close to realization, both of which were tied to recreational areas in the city. The first was in Vera Park where construction of the line was halted at a very early stage, leaving only a small portion of the station building platform visible today. This line held great potential to transport passengers from a scenic promontory at the northern edge of the park dramatically down to a landing on the opposite (left) bank of the Mtkvari river, close to the current location of the Marjanishvili Bridge. Similarly, the half-constructed cable car line close to the top of Kus Tba/Turtle Lake would have connected the lower and the upper parts of the Tbilisi Open Air Ethnographic Museum with one another. But today only the leftover relics of these proposals can be found.

Perhaps the least-remembered Soviet-era cable car line in Tbilisi is that which passed through Mziuri park in Vake. The park itself was the 1970s dream project of Georgian writer Nodar Dumbadze who aimed to create a unique space for children to play along the Vere River gorge. In contrast with Tbilisi's other more expansive Soviet-era cable car lines that cut across vast geographic distances and navigated extreme topographic conditions, the Mziuri park line was much humbler and confined solely within the park, quickly connecting the lower banks of the Vere River with an area close to the park's main entrance. According to the park's landscape architect, Irakli Maskharashvili, the Soviet city administration had intended to expand the recreation space further into the gorge and had also aimed to extend the cable car line up into the hilltop recreational settlements of Tskneti and Akhladaba.[14] With the collapse of the Soviet Union, these expansions never came to fruition and the existing line was decommissioned. Following Georgian independence, the number of annual visitors to Mziuri park diminished due to poor maintenance, making the line's reactivation unnecessary. As of 2016, the park is being updated and redeveloped, albeit with no clear plans to reconnect the cable car line.[15]

Urban Regeneration and the Return of Tbilisi's Aerial Connections   As of August 2016, the engineering consulting firm Systra has carried out an extensive public transport opportunity study on behalf of Tbilisi City Hall, exploring the feasibility of implementing a series of new cable transit corridors.[16] These proposed corridors combine existing cable car infrastructure with new construction and in some cases coincide with the initiatives set forth in former Soviet plans. Due to the considerable urban transformations that have taken place since cable car decommissioning in the 1990s, the study suggests that the majority of the existing lines be replaced with new, re-situated infrastructure. With the introduction of these new transit nodes the fate of the existing station buildings remains unclear.

A key specification of the ten proposed routes is that they meet either the city's mass transit and/or leisure needs and that they often represent a »feeder« function, plugging riders into the rest of the city's existing public transport network.[17] As with their Soviet predecessors, such connections hold the potential to greatly increase the outdoor recreation spaces of Tbilisi and promise to better link the city to its more natural peripheries.

In 2012, signs of the reactivation of the city's cable car network could be seen concretely in the construction of a new gondola line linking

tbilisi/22406-msheneblobam-sheidzleba-kus-tbis-sabagiro-sheitsiros.html.
14 Kakhurashvili, I., ახალი »მზიური« – სივრცე ყველასათვის. Focus – ფოკუსი, accessed January 12, 2016, www.focus.ge/nomris-thema/article/9218-akhali-mziuri-sivrce-yvelasathvis.
15 Agenda.ge, *A playground city for children: New Mziuri project revitalises flood-ravaged park, accessed March 17, 2016, www.agenda.ge/news/54206/eng.

16 Systra, Tbilisi Cable Transit Master Plan.
17 Amongst the ten corridors, four have been tailored primarily to mass transit purposes (Samgori-Vasizubani; Vazha Phsavela-Nutsubidze Plato; Sarajishvili-Zghvisubani; Akhmeteli Theatre- Zghvisubani), two to primarily leisure purposes (Rustaveli-Mtatsminda; Vake Park-Turtle Lake), and four combine the two purposes (University-Bagebi-Tskneti; Vazha Phsavela-Bagebi-Tskneti; Didube-Vashlijvari-Lisi Lake; Station Square-Lotkini-Tbilisi Sea). These proposed lines

Map of the city's existing and proposed cable car lines.

Proposed line – Soviet (unbuilt)
Underground metro
Proposed line – Post-Soviet (unbuilt)
Soviet line – re-activated (built)
Post-Soviet new line (built)
Soviet line – inactive (built)

Rike Park on the left bank of the Mtkvari river to the ancient hilltop fortress of Narikala.[18] This gondola was introduced as part of the broader 2009 *New Life for Old Tbilisi* urban regeneration initiative implemented by the UNM Government, which brought about rapid and controversial change to the eastern neighborhoods of the city, often harming the existing authenticity of Old Tbilisi.[19] *New Life for Old Tbilisi* involved the strategic upgrading and beautification of highly-visible areas of the old town – many of which were observable from the scenic gondola ride above. In contrast to Tbilisi's other publicly-owned cable car lines, the Rike Park-Narikala line is privately-run. The primary purpose of this line has been touristic development and it does not address the city's broader public transportation concerns.

The desire to revive cable car infrastructure in Tbilisi can also be seen in the $1,3 billion proposal for *Panorama Tbilisi*, a mega-project which was announced in 2014, funded by the former Prime Minister of Georgia, Bidzina Ivanishvili.[20] The project primarily consists of four hotel complexes situated throughout Tbilisi's old town and its immediate mountainous areas in Sololaki.[21] A mixture of hotels and business centers are proposed to be connected to one another via cable car lines, enabling users to move between them. Despite initial construction on one of the hotel projects, widespread controversy surrounding the scope of the project and its infringement upon natural and heritage areas has halt-

further include consideration of possible phasing strategies for the mass transit corridors to extend up into mountainous regions for leisure purposes in the future. Such is the case with the University-Bagebi line and the Vazha Phsavela-Bagebi line, which could both be extended up to Tskneti. Likewise, the Station Square-Lotkini line has the potential to be extended up to Tbilisi Sea (Systra, Tbilisi Cable Transit Master Plan, 8).

18 Tabula, თბილისში კიდევ ერთი საბაგირო გზა აშენდება.
19 Salukvadze, J. and Golubchikov, O., »City as a geopolitics: Tbilisi, Georgia – A globalizing metropolis in a turbulent region.« In Cities, 52, 39-54, accessed April 8, 2018, doi: www.dx.doi.org/10.1016/j.cities. 2015.11.013
20 Ibid.,52.
21 Ioseliani, »Panorama Development Project«. In Photos: Citizens Say »No«. Georgia Today. Accessed

ed further development.[22] As of early 2017, it is not clear whether the project will ever be implemented in its entirety.

In contrast to the tourism focus of these privatized cable car lines, the publicly-owned and operated Chavchavadze Avenue-Kus Tba/Turtle Lake line was re-opened on October 2016 and directly integrated into the existing fare system of Tbilisi's public transit.[23] A key difficulty facing the reconstruction effort, however, was a conflicting proposal for a high-rise residential building situated directly in the flight path. Although eventually the cable car's reconstruction won out over that of the building's, construction blocking cable car flight paths is a common concern for re-commissioning across the city.[24] For example, buildings constructed inside the flight path of the 1978 lower station building at Nutsubidze Street have rendered this particular site entirely obsolete.

At the same time, former station buildings, such as that of the Nut-subidze Street-Lisi Lake line, have evolved to take on new lives of their own. Since the time of this line's original construction in August of 1978, the lower station building has experienced a range of ad-hoc alterations and additions. The building's lower level now houses a convenience store, money exchange, and a hair salon and is so camouflaged within its commercial programming that it can barely be recognized as an original piece of Soviet-era aerial transportation at all.

The upper station building at Lisi Lake.

The former upper station building of the Nutsubidze Street-Lisi Lake line tells a different story. Remotely nestled amongst a forest of pine trees and situated a good five-minute walk from any of the main recreational attractions around the Lisi Lake, its impressive monolithic form remains mostly hidden from civilization. Designed by Georgian architect, Varlam Khechinashvili, the building is elegantly white and centered around an open-air cascading spiral staircase. Graffiti art is one of the few clues of its abandonment.

Cable Transit Corridors: Inter-Urban Connections in the City   In contrast to the more vertical, recreational routes that linked the lower urban core of Tbilisi to natural spaces in the city's scenic mountainous vicinity, a number of cable

April 8, 2018, www.georgiatoday.ge/news/691/Panorama-Development-Project,-in-Photos%3A-Citizens-Say-%22No%22.
22 CBW, *Panorama Tbilisi, Supporters, Objectors and their Arguments*. In Caucasus Business Week, accessed May 19, 2015, www.cbw.ge/business/panorama-tbilisi-supporters-objectors-and-their-arguments/.
23 Tbilisi City Hall, *Turtle Lake renewed ropeway opened, accessed* 2016, www.tbilisi.gov.ge/news/2990?lang=en

24 Systra, Tbilisi Cable Transit Master Plan, p.49.

car lines built during the Soviet era were intended to serve as horizontal daily commuter lines. One that operated in this fashion was from Didube to Saakadze Square, constructed in 1961. It ran horizontally over the Mtkvari River in the south-west of the city and its primary function was to provide a direct connection between these neighborhoods, prior to the Vakhushti Bagrationi Bridge's construction in 1972. In 1970 this line was the busiest of Tbilisi's aerial transport lines, serving up to 617,000 passengers annually.[25] The line functioned for about ten years until its decommissioning. Later in the 1990s, the vacant station buildings were sold-off to private interests. The building at Saakadze Square now acts as the office space for a shipping company, while the right bank station has been overwhelmingly absorbed by the chaos of the Eliava construction market. With the development of the Vakhushti Bridge, there is no longer a need for an aerial connection in this location.

Similar to the Didube-Saakadze Square line, the State University-Bagebi line horizontally commuted students from dormitory buildings across the Vere River gorge to their campus. This line was constructed in 1983 and was in use for roughly eight years until decommissioning. Following Georgian independence, the under-utilized university dormitory buildings took on a range of new inhabitants including *Internally Displaced Persons* (IDPs) seeking informal accommodation. A nearby pedestrian foot bridge across the gorge currently serves as the sole crossing point between the two sides of the river in this area. In line with the recommendations of the Systra report, reconstruction on this line started in 2016. Its station buildings are slated to be in working condition by as early as 2018.[26] As such, the line will once again connect the dormitory area with the State University side of the river, further plugging into the new 2017 University metro station.[27] The reactivation of this line is the first example of Tbilisi City Hall constructing an integrated inter-modal transit link as part of the city's broader strategy toward public transport since Soviet times. Similar plans have been suggested for reactivating the Samgori-Vazisubani line across town to the east for inter-modal transit purposes.

The IDP inhabited upper station building in Vazisubani.

The Samgori-Vazisubani line was the last line to be completed in the Soviet era. Built in 1986 in one of the most populated areas of Tbilisi, it began operation in 1988.[28] The line carried thousands of residents from the numerous Soviet *microraions* of Vazisubani down to Samgori where they could easily access the city's broader transportation network at the Samgori Metro station and Navtlugi transport hub. Today, both station buildings are in serious disrepair, but the cable lines hanging between them remain aerially suspended with two passenger carts still attached: a scene highly reminiscent of the 1990s when most of the decommissioned lines still boasted carts precariously dangling above. Today, both the Samgori and Vazisubani station buildings have come to blend in with their adjacent urban fabric, yet two large, rusted, metal-frame support masts are still overwhelmingly visible. Proposals for the reactivation of this line recommend entirely new station buildings, with the lower station moved much closer to the Samgori metro.

As with the obsolete station buildings on Nutsubidze Street, at Didube Metro, and in Saakadze Square, the abandoned buildings for this line show signs of innovative reuse and transformation. In the upper

25 Georgian Soviet Encyclopedia, 1981, 143.
26 City.Kvira.Ge, თსუ-ს მაღლივი კორპუსის ბაგებთან დამაკავშირებელი საბაგირო რეაბილიტაციია მალე დასრულდება.
27 Systra, Tbilisi Cable Transit Master Plan, 8.
28 Kverenchkiladze, R., შიგასაქალაქო ტრანსპორტი.

station building at Vazisubani, the building is currently a make-shift home for IDPs.[29] The occupants have made minor adaptations to the exterior of the building, including boarding up the windows and filling in the large wall slots used to receive the tensioned cables. In an opening on the upper receiving platform, two mature fig trees now grow. Plant life further spills out onto the platform, camouflaging its deteriorated surface in lush greenery.

There are other signs of ad-hoc building use and inhabitation at the Vazisubani station, including stenciled graffiti produced by the Tbilisi-based art duo *Sadarismelia* (Mariam Natroshvili and Detu Jintcharadze) that reads »IGNORE« in English. The duo describes their work as being »inspired by stories and biographies of places and people,« and that their interventions are »interested in disappearing knowledge, invisible people, forgotten places, and ignored spaces.«[30] At Vazisubani, this leaves open interpretations of »IGNORE« being in reference to the city's Soviet cable car network or the housing needs of its protracted internally displaced (IDP) population. Similar stenciled graffiti by *Sadarismelia* can be found on other Soviet-era abandoned structures, including on the Lisi Lake upper station building which has been branded with »ERROR«. The Mziuri lower station building has »NOT NOW« written on it, and across town, the Mukhatgverdi cemetery crematory reads »PLEASE WAIT«.

The construction of a new high-rise apartment building directly adjacent to the Vazisubani upper station signals future change for the area. With the proposal to create an alternate new mid-level station building further into the built fabric of Vazisubani, the current IDP residents may be spared eviction, but it is uncertain what other future change might bring. Despite Tbilisi City Hall's announcements in 2015 to use the Samgori-Vazisubani line as a pilot for the urban cable car project,[31] work has yet to commence and government attention toward cable car development has instead been focused on projects in the core of the city.

Throughout the past century, cable car transportation lines have played an integral yet ever-evolving role in the urban development of Tbilisi. Early Soviet lines aimed to connect the city to its peripheral mountainsides for recreational purposes. These lines were then complemented in the 1980s by aerial transit corridors that transcended horizontal boundaries in urban areas and connected to transit stations. Today, the slow reintroduction of cable car lines appears to be driven by desires to offer tourism experiences, fitting with Tbilisi City Hall's overall strategy to develop a tourist city. This can be seen in the local government's prioritization of the lines from Rike Park to Narikala and from Rustaveli to Mtatsminda, but also in the dramatic proposal for cable car connections in the *Panorama Tbilisi* project. The opportunity study produced by Systra Consultants in 2016 offers hope that the use of cable car lines might also be extended for public transportation purposes. With the ever-increasing luxury development and gentrification of Tbilisi's downtown core, such connections could support local residents who rely more on public transportation to access downtown. Because of this, new cable car lines that connect to transit networks should be a top priority of the government. Given the undulating landscape and rocky geography of Tbilisi, there is great potential to develop cable car lines that better integrate remote

29 Secessionist conflict between Georgia and its autonomous regions of South Ossetia and Abkhazia following independence in 1991 resulted in a humanitarian crisis that drove displaced populations into the capital city where they sought refuge in abandoned buildings. In many areas, some twenty-five years later, Georgia's IDPs continue to inhabit abandoned structures.
30 For more on the work of Sadarismelia, see their website: www.sadarismelia.com/

31 Giely, J.-M., Tbilisi Sustainable Urban Transport Strategy, accessed April 8, 2018, www.mdf.org. ge/storage/assets/file/documents%202016/mur-tazi/Strategic%20Paper%20Report%20PDF%20 Geo(18_03_2016)/Strategic%20Paper%20Report%20final%20ENG.pdf, iii.

areas with public transport, making the city overall a more accessible place for residents. Cable car transportation continues to be a unique marker of the identity of Tbilisi and a particular register of its beautiful undulating geography. As the city continuously undergoes its post-independence transformations, the abandoned relics of its cable car past will now stand as de-facto monuments alongside the cable cars of its future.

3 Publics and Counter-Publics[1]

1   Title borrows from Michael Warner's groundbreaking work of the same name: Zone Books, 2002

a

b

c

e

f

g

h

j

k

Publics and Counter-Publics

Family, work, food, health. As the structuring pillars of everyday life, it comes as no surprise that these are the recurring categories in the deep archive of public life held in the National Archives. Here we have the drama of the everyday at its most playful – and at times most theatrical. From the ritual of the bath-house to the ritual of the supra, from the choreography of children's play to the choreography of the domestic, the range of this selection reminds us that society – as a specifically dense constellation of individuals – was always the promised stake in the grand Soviet pageant. Public life – of the lived or the representational kind – is perhaps where we can best measure the densities and distances of transition.

a   Typical Georgian massage in the sulfur baths of Old Tbilisi, 1971.

b   Voluntary workers out during a rest-day in Tbilisi, 1978.

c   Children's playground near the Mtkvari river bank, 1970.

d   Grape cultivation and harvesting at the edge of Tbilisi, 1984.

e   Renting a flat in Tbilisi, 1968.

f   Voluntary workers out during a rest-day in Tbilisi, 1978.

g   Grape cultivation and harvesting at the edge of Tbilisi, 1984.

h   Housewarming in the newly built Gldani district, 1980.

i   Wedding on a collective farm in Akhalsopheli village in the Kvareli region of Kakheti, 1964.

j   Compact cassette workshop at the Tbilisi recording studio with the head of the production laboratory, Ivan Salukvadze, 1973.

k   Grape cultivation and harvesting at the edge of Tbilisi, 1984.

l   A new year in a new apartment, Tbilisi, 1974.

The Chinese Butterfly Monster

Ben Knight

Genadi is not impressed. »Look, it's made for Chinese people,« our Georgian driver laughs, standing in the door frame of one of the apartment blocks. For emphasis he does a mohican-hand on his head to demonstrate how small the door is. »This is the front door!« he exclaims, exasperated. Next he walks around the outside walls, where he pauses to reach out a fingernail and pick a flake of plaster from a corner. »This is a new building?« he wonders, before barking a hollow laugh.

From a distance, the buildings in this vast, brand new housing estate look quite nice. At least they do compared to the unforgiving grubbiness of the Soviet housing blocks that make up the nearby Tbilisi suburb. To me, lacking Genadi's expert fingernail, the outline of these bright red roofs rising against the windy Caucasian steppe in a pleasingly regular pattern look kind of handsome, even Parisian. That's not the only incongruity here: in the distance, beyond a spanking new four-lane superhighway that currently marks the border of this hyper-modern development, you can make out boy-shepherds riding bareback as they coral small herds of sheep and cows across the bare brown hills.

This is Hualing Tbilisi Sea New City, or at least the first part of it, a vast construction site on the shore of the Tbilisi Sea, a poorly-named lake just beyond the crest of the hills on the outskirts of Georgia's capital. In fact, the Hualing Group is only just getting started. The three-billion dollar corporation from Urumqi, northwestern China, has colossal ambitions for this apron of unused land on the edge of these vast and ancient Caucasian steppes. A video the Group released on YouTube paints a CGI picture of what's in store for the shepherd cowboys' pasture land on the other side of the highway – it's a 420-hectare concrete butterfly that will one day lay its wings across the steppes. In seven years' time, the video promises that the area will have become a spectacular suburb, as comforting and prosperous as something out of Steven Spielberg: the video shows computer-generated children (safely helmeted) roller-blading around a fountain featuring a ring of leaping stone horses, while people mill around, shopping in the sunshine.

Once it's finished, Hualing Tbilisi will have the shape of a 420-hectare concrete butterfly that sits just next to Tbilisi Sea.

The sales brochure also promises there will be an urban array as complete as a Playmobil set: a school, a kindergarten, a hospital, a police station, a fire brigade. The people living in the butterfly will be divided by class – someone should probably tell Genadi that the high-rises he picked at are just the cheaper part of the district (though they start at $635 per square metres, in a country where the average monthly salary is $285) but one day there will be smaller apartment buildings and even, so the video says, villas surrounded by dense thickets of trees.

But who is going to live here, this place that locals have suspiciously begun to call »Chinatown«? That nickname stuck because of a rumour started by Jondi Bagaturia, leader of a leftist nationalist party called the Georgian Troupe who claimed that the government signed a secret deal allowing the Hualing Group to fly in thousands of Chinese immigrants to live in the new settlement. It was a highly effective rumour, which nourished the usual fears – but it wasn't true.

»There was even a number – 126,000 Chinese,« remembers Tinatin Shishinashvili, whose main job as Hualing's public relations spokeswoman has been to assuage these nationalist fears about Chinese en-

croachment. »But then everybody has confirmed that we haven't such plans, that the project is quite open. It's a commercial development, and anybody who is interested and who wants to buy can buy these flats.«

Shishinashvili, who has now mastered languages in three different alphabets, is sitting on an olive green plastic armchair in the foyer of the Hotel Preference (the centrepiece and currently the only humming place in Tbilisi Sea New City). She simultaneously embodies and stands out from her surroundings. There's a huge painting of a Chinese flower behind the reception desk, and businessmen from a trade fair promoting »Partnerships for Competitiveness, Innovation, and Cybersecurity« are hovering around us, greeting each other loudly in their suits. Beside us, a sign at the entrance to the hotel restaurant instructs us to »Be Chic«. Shishinashvili fits in.

So if it's not 126,000 Chinese people, who exactly is going to move here? »You mean because Georgia does not have a strong internal market or consumption?« asks Shishinashvili.

»Er, yeah.«

»That's a good question.« Firstly, she explains, the mortgages are going at zero percent, if you make a 25-percent down payment. »The sales are going well, many flats have already been sold,« she says. Yes, but even so, I wonder – Georgia has a 12 or 13 percent unemployment rate. Considering that the population of the whole country is only 4,5 million, and you want 30,000 people to move here, there's still a lot of buyers to find.

At this point Shishinashvili admits that the Hualing Group has already sold eight high-rise blocks »for a non-commercial price« to the

116

Entrance of the »Hôtels & Préférence« Hualing Tbilisi.

117

government to house refugees from Abkhazia and South Ossetia. These *Internally Displaced Persons* are stragglers left in limbo after Russia's invasion of Georgia in 2008, a shift in the international balance that gave many western investors the willies about the Caucasus region, and so opened the door for Hualing's Butterfly to settle. Exploiting the West's Putin paranoia, China became Georgia's biggest single investor, with Chinese investors most interested in the Georgian construction industry and agricultural sector.

Not only that, according to data from Geostat, the Hualing Group was the biggest investor of the first nine months of 2014, and the Tbilisi Sea New City represents just the largest of its five big projects. Looking at the other four, it's pretty obvious that housing is not its main concern – in the city of Kutaisi to the west there is now a Hualing Free Industrial Zone, a 36-hectare industrial and logistics hub where companies are already processing wood, stone and metal and manufacturing furniture and mattresses. Meanwhile, Hualing has acquired 20-year licenses to harvest timber and stone from around the country. To help grease all these wheels, not to mention the mortgages for the new homes, Hualing has also bought 90 percent of the Georgian Basisbank.

But even all these deals do not cover the reach of Hualing's ambitions. »Hualing Group was aiming not just at Georgia itself, but to have Georgia as the main platform in the region,« says Shishinashvili. »Many investors are interested in Georgia's free trade agreements with different countries, like CIS countries, Turkey, European Union countries, who will give them the opportunity to export their goods as made in Georgia.«

This all makes historical sense. Both Urumqi and Tbilisi used to be on the Silk Road, a point that gets mentioned a lot in the promotional materials. It also appeals to Wato Tsereteli. Wato is an artist, lecturer, and the founder of the Centre of Contemporary Art in Tbilisi, where he sits now, with a converted warehouse full of busy young artists around him. His bald head, his robe-like duffel coat, and his irascible insistence on drawing a deep yet sweeping conclusion out of every question, combine to make his earnestness even more monkish. »It's good, I think it's good that the Chinese are building that up there – of course, why not?« he says. »We have never had a bourgeoisie, it just never happened here. And Georgia is not a European country, it doesn't have a European language – it has its own small language.«

For Wato, Chinese economic expansion into Georgia is a counterweight to the cultural globalization that the West is forcing on his country. »We're like a gate between civilization – the West, Europe, Russia, the Middle East, Asia – Tbilisi was a very important point in the Silk Road, not just because people stopped here, but because many products were exchanged here and distributed. What always fed us was everything – East, West, North, South – everything. But at the moment we only look to Europe. It's not healthy.«

Genadi, his fingers still in the cracks of one of the new high-rises, probably wouldn't call the Butterfly healthy. By this time, he has found more building flaws in the commercial area further up the imaginary insect's torso. Apart from the hotel, the gym, and 20 or-so blocks of flats, the only part of the Butterfly currently functioning is a huge wholesale

retail park that will one day be centred around a 110,000-square-meter shopping mall (now a building site that takes minutes to drive past).

Chinese construction workers in front of the hotel.

At the moment this retail park is collected in a complex of barracks, spread across the dusty steppe in a grid of neat rectangles. These low, hastily constructed buildings form a drive-through wholesalers' mall where cheap products are arranged by item, so traders can come along in trucks and load up a hundred motorbikes, or a million plastic Spidermen, or ten million cigarettes (all made in China, naturally). Then they drive on to Istanbul or Tehran or Volgograd, depending on which pass you take out of Georgia's mountains. As you walk around this mass of choking commercial trash, silently shadowed by some Chinese store managers, you realize this is what Georgia's future economy will be based on. The quality might be low, but as Joe Stalin, Georgia's most infamous child, once said, »Quantity has a quality all its own.«

119

Tbilisi Sea Hualing Plaza international trade center is a 150,000-square-meter exhibition hall and warehousing center opened in 2017. The site currently marks the spatial edge of Tbilisi's urban development, with multinational businesses colliding with longstanding land-uses of the area.

Contentious Politics[1]
Lela Rekhviashvili

This is the story with which my doctoral supervisor, Professor Béla Greskovits, starts his course of lectures on social movements: in the early 1990s, Béla and several other scholars from Eastern Europe were invited to the United States. It was during this visit that he learned of the American interpretation of the reasons for *perestroika* and the eventual collapse of the Soviet Union: it was primarily due to Reagan's efforts. To Eastern European researchers, on the other hand, the majority of whom had fought hard to achieve transformation in their respective socialist countries by the end of the 1980s, it sounded ironic and embarrassing: as if the risk they and their compatriots had taken, all the effort they had made to mobilize masses to achieve regime change, had been quite irrelevant. It was at this moment that Béla found it important to study social movements, realizing how partial existing elite-centered interpretations were.

This story reminds us, researchers and members of various civil movements, of the simple but nevertheless significant conviction that citizens' collective effort can bring about change – be it social, political, or economic – at both large and local scales. While challenging, it is vitally important for both researchers of social movements and members of the movements themselves to assess the achievements and influences rendered by their actions. My own assessment is that the most important achievements reached by various urban protest movements in Georgia include the following: the introduction of the new, creative forms of political expression; new forms of socializing in public spaces; and the practice of articulating demands during negotiations. These new forms and repertoires are both a *demand* for the politicization of urban space as well as an *invention* of everyday forms of appropriation involved in the production and reproduction of space. In this, we would do well to recall Robert Park's call to claim our rights to the city:

> »The question – what kind of a city we want – cannot be regarded separately from what kind of social ties, relationship with nature, lifestyle, technologies and aesthetic values we are striving for. A claim on the city is larger than a mere individual access to urban resources: it is a right to transform ourselves alongside the change the city undergoes. It is also a collective, rather than individual right, as such transformation is inevitably dependent on the collective effort forming the process of urbanization. I would like to say that the right to create or transform our cities and ourselves is one of the most valuable and most ignored of the human rights«.[2]

My aim here is to discuss the achievements and challenges of urban protest movements in Georgia.[3] I am writing this article in early March 2016 and it would be impossible not to mention one of the key events in the history of social movements in independent Georgia – the 16-day strike of the Tkibuli miners. The miners went on strike in February 2016 demanding improvements in working conditions and salary increases from their employer, the Georgian Indistrial Group (GIG), who operates two mines in the small industrial town of Tkibuli in western Georgia. Without underestimating the power of previous instances of cooperation between worker and young-leftist organizations, the solidarity displayed by various groups with the workers in Tkibuli, and the collective involvement in

1   This text was previously published as »Civil Society and Political Society in Urban Contentious Politics« in the anthology *The city is ours! Urban protests and politics in Tbilisi* undertaken by the Heinrich Böll Foundation, Southern Caucasian Regional Office, 2017. We thank the editors for permission to reprint an edited and shortened version in English.
2   Park, R., collection of translations »The City, A Critical Introduction«, In Asabashvili, L, ed., transl. Ghiorghi Kevlishvili (1967).

3   My observations are largely based on personal research on informal economic practices in Tbilisi as well as the empirical material offered in David Sichinava, David Chigholashvili, Nino Zazanashvili and Esma Berlikishvili's above-mentioned anthology *The city is ours!*, 2016.

communicating, problematizing and politicizing the values of the strike, was unprecedented.

I raise the case of the miner's strike not because of its timeliness nor with the ambition to systematically analyze events in Tkibuli; rather, I am using the case because it helps us identify key questions that are relevant to the study of urban protest movements more generally. In what ways can we understand the Tkibuli strike as an urban protest? What are the parameters and characteristics of urban protests more generally? How might we interpret the outcomes and achievements of this and other urban protests based on the framing motivations of the movement? What are the challenges associated with mobilizing around urban problems and the movements to bring about change?

Theory and Definitions: Place of Urban Movements among Other Social Movements So, what is an urban protest movement and what makes it different from other kinds of movement? Following urban theorist Hans Pruijt, urban movements can be defined as »social movements through which citizens attempt to achieve some control over their urban environment. The urban environment comprises the built environment, the social fabric of the city, and the local political processes«[4]. If we can understand urban movements – like environmental, feminist, or other focused movements – as a more specific form of social movement, it is perhaps also productive to define this form of collective action as well. Here we can identify social movements as the »collective challenges by people with common purposes and solidarity in sustained interaction with elites, opponents and authorities.«[5] The space of collective political struggle in which this interaction and opposition takes place can be understood as the practice of *contentious politics*, a term that Tilly and Tarrow employ to describe the »episodic, public, collective interaction« between protesters and the state. Therefore, where contentious politics is made up of diverse episodes of contention (such as protests, strikes, demonstrations, hunger strikes, petitions, etc.), social movements can be understood as the framing strategy for the sustained practice of contentious politics and the capacity to create collective identity, interpret injustice, and construct relatively stable social networks.

The Tkibuli miners' strike demonstrates how difficult it is to draw a clear line between different types of movements, and how the structures of social movements often combine several forms in themselves. On the one hand, the Tkibuli strike, with its demands for improved working conditions and a 40% wage increase, can be classified as a workers' movement. On the other, the town of Tkibuli and its inhabitants are directly linked to, and sometimes even dependent on, the miner's rights and remuneration. With the collective support of the town's inhabitants, then, the miners' strike was clearly both an urban protest and a workers' protest – with the miner's actions being relevant for both the fabric of the town and for local political processes.

The next question is of course how to understand social movements. When and why do they take place and when and why do they succeed or fail? One of the most significant theoretical frameworks to study social movements is the *political opportunity theory*[6]. This framework

4 Pruijt, H., Urban movements. In G. Ritzer (Ed.), *The Blackwell Encyclopedia of Sociology* (Oxford, UK, Malden, USA and Carlton, Australia: Blackwell Publishing Ltd, 2007), accessed April 4, 2018, https://repub.eur.nl/pub/19231/Urban%20Movements%20preprint.pdf.
5 McAdam, D., Tarrow, S.G. and Tilly, C., *Dynamics of contention* (Cambridge, UK: Cambridge University Press, 2001); Tarrow, S.G., *Power in movements: social movements and contentious politics* (Cambridge: Cambridge University Press, 1998).

takes into account structural and institutional contexts on the one hand, and the initiative demonstrated by citizens on the other. In other words, the study of social movements is an attempt to articulate how relevant political involvement of individuals, and particularly their collective mobilization, is in a given structural environment. According to this approach, the capability to achieve social mobilization and a group's goals varies by political contexts. Political contexts, in turn, may vary across space and over time. On the one hand, social movements are stronger in democratic or less repressive political contexts. On the other hand, political opportunities for mobilization can vary over time even within the same regime (e.g. when an authoritarian regime is weaker or before elections).

Notwithstanding the relevance of political opportunities theory, before simply applying this theory we must be alert to its weaknesses and challenges. The most evident challenge is that political opportunities theory is primarily rooted in a specifically western experience of social mobilization. Despite recently being applied to a range of global regions, dominant social movements theorization has taken place in and about western political environments. Importantly, apart from the difficulty in applying the existing concepts to non-western contexts, the reliance on social movements' theory may also *conceal* numerous politically relevant processes. In some regions there may not be any organized and viable social movements at all, or they may be scarcely represented, but this does not mean that their citizens have no possibility to influence political and social processes on the local level.

Numerous, alternative theoretical frameworks have emerged to study movements that are politically and socially significant but that have remained invisible to western theories. For the purposes of this article, I would highlight Parta Chatterjee's concept of *political society*, or the collective action of marginalized groups, which he draws in distinction to *civic society*, or the mode of activism and engagement sometimes enjoyed by a relatively privileged middle class.[7] In his description of political society, Chatterjee observes the interaction of citizens who are poor, without rights, illegally represented or otherwise marginalized by politicians on the local level – an interaction through which the political society nonetheless manages to achieve some benefits and legitimacy of action with varying success. The line dividing political and civil modes of involvement is often drawn by the legal or institutional framework in which they are exercised. While a civil society respects the existing institutional frame and operates within it, political society always tries to find creative forms to overcome and modify these institutional structure as the very source of inequality and marginalization.

In line with Chatterjee, I would argue that when thinking of social movements and political contention in Georgia it is important to think beyond visible cases of collective mobilization and look into the everyday practices of marginalized citizens. Whereas less visible movements may not be characterized by the forms of collective engagement defined through existing norms of contentious politics (such as frames, narratives, identity formation, solidity of formal or informal social networks) such movements are often implicitly, rather than explicitly, coordinated and collective. As you will see below, consideration of lessapparent forms of

6 To be more precise, there were more researchers that laid the foundation of the political opportunity theory, but Tilly and Tarrow stood out as the best-known and defining authors.
7 Chatterjee, P., *The politics of the governed: reflections on popular politics in most of the world* (New York: Columbia University Press, 2004).

mobilization is central for the analysis of Georgian urban movements and the challenges they face.

Challenges: Invisibility of Forms Engaged in Creation of Urban Space   For urban protest movements, political mobilization stands out as the most acute of numerous interrelated challenges. The challenges associated with achieving fast and large-scale mobilization becomes particularly important in a context where powerful actors willing to employ and exploit urban space are effectively and even aggressively involved. Berikishvili and Sichinava note: »The state, the investor, and the influential citizen are always mobilized.«[8] Activists can see for themselves that the passive stance taken by the majority of ordinary citizens, coupled with the relative social homogeneity of the small active groups, are interconnected difficulties. So while mobilization is the primary hurdle, our research shows there to be three related challenges through which urban protest movements are still working. The first challenge relates to the difficulty urban protest movements face in creating an inclusive narrative around an urban agenda that invites a broader coalition of citizens to identify with the issues being contested. This leads us to the second challenge, which is the practical and conceptual linking of urban problems to broader social and political challenges. Finally, the third, somewhat paradoxical challenge is a general hesitance on the part of activists to overly politicize their protests.

My view is that these difficulties arise because existing urban protest movements are unable to perceive the relevance of a range of political actions taking place by less-than-visible and often marginalized groups. As it stands now, urban activists usually identify the problem of mobilization in the lack of involvement on behalf of the majority of citizens. My counter argument, in turn, is that urban activists *themselves* are unable to perceive the diversity of various politically relevant actions. In order to clarify my point, I suggest we look at the suburbs – specifically Gldani. I choose Gldani as a good example of the production and transformation of urban space by citizens, where one can see citizen involvement in the physical and social transformation of space much more clearly than in the center. The center is a much more visible, controlled, and exploited space for the projection of national narratives by existing political forces. The outskirts appear to be less relevant for such purpose, and as a result are open to more active transformation by citizens. Residents do not only modify Soviet housing infrastructure, but public space is also intensively used for trade and diverse forms of socialization. Even garages in Gldani are turned into sites of exchange, providing space for basic services, bakeries, or shops.

Similar transformations of urban space, alongside the everyday struggles of those involved, are consistently ignored by both academics and urban activists. Moreover, such cases of appropriation are often perceived negatively even among urban activist circles. For example, the way in which *marshutka*[9] drivers pilot their vehicles, the scale at which private parking-lot wardens have appropriated open spaces in the city, and the occupation of pavement by street vendors, are all practices that are regularly stigmatized and criticized. However, seeing these everyday forms as contentious productions of urban space, and recognizing their

8 See »Transformation of Urban Protests« in this book, 173.
9 A system of shared, route-based taxies, complementing public transport in Tbilisi.

potential political relevance, could well be an opportunity for urban activists to acknowledge the conflict and pave the way towards a dialogue.

Besides everyday practices of claiming and appropriating urban space, numerous episodes of collective mobilization remain in the shadows of more celebrated urban movements centered around cultural heritage and environmental issues. For example, the mobilization of internally displaced persons, the mobilization of street vendors, rallies to demand the regulation of creditor/eviction cases, and certain attempts of the evicted to occupy urban space, are, while unsystematic, still on the urban agenda. Some of these struggles, especially the struggle of street vendors and internally displaced persons, have, to my knowledge, never enjoyed mass solidarity or support; however, these episodes of contentious politics are extremely important instances of citizens exercising their right to the city. They look more like struggles of the political society described by Chatterjee than the mobilizations of civil society. The rule of law, peaceful organization, and the protection of property rights is not a priority for marginalized groups. For a victim of the existing institutional framework, breaking through this frame and bending it to suit her interests is a form of struggle. For as long as I have studied the problems facing street vendors, I can assert that the vendors' struggle has been a struggle to gain political voice. Indeed, vendors initially tried to mobilize within the normative frameworks of civil society and to stage numerous acts of collective protest; however, facing extensive repressions they shifted strategy toward a creative bending of state imposed exclusion from public spaces. Here, they tried to redefine the existing rules through daily confrontations and negotiations with representatives of the state – be it the police or city hall supervisors.

I personally believe that these acts of resistance must be counted as valid ways of producing contentious politics, and are sometimes even more critical than the activism undertaken within civil society. Just like other urban movements, street vendors also fight against the marketization and commodification of urban space. There are numerous other examples of social movements in the Georgian political environment that may not be regarded as specifically urban, but that try to articulate their claim over the city. For example, we must include the attempts by the LGBT community to occupy public space and increase their public visibility on May 17, 2013 and 2015, the various protests of the Invisibles[10] in May 2014, as well as numerous urban interventions by feminist groups, as important efforts to access and transform urban space.[11] In other words, there are a great number of actors and movements engaged in the production of urban space and in the identification of problems related to the repressive rules governing its articulation. One of the challenges facing existing urban movements is to properly perceive how relevant some of the less visible, counter movements are.

While the central problem lies in the inability of the majority of urban activists to see as valid the actions of diverse, if marginalized, groups acting outside the bounds of conventional forms of political mobilization, another problem lies in the conflicts, real or potential, between the interests of these two groups in contentious urban politics. Notwithstanding this confrontation, it will be impossible to align the political society with

10 As the LGBT rally was brutally attacked on May 17, 2013 and the state largely failed in assuring the participants' security, the LGBT community decided against staging a public rally a year after, on May 17, 2014. However, different groups of activists then organized a series of protests without physically appearing in public spaces. These started with a »protest for Invisibles and against invisibility«. An installation at Pushkin Square, the location where a LGBT rally was violently attacked in 2013, laid out hundreds of shoes representing those community members for whom it was not safe to appear in public spaces. The series of invisible protests then followed this installation, with a LGBT flag painted on stairs near Pushkin square and notes containing anti-homophobic messages spread around the city (see more here: www.dfwatch.net/protests-in-support-of-the-invisibles-11622-28790). 11 The LGBT community in Georgia had been organizing small-scale rallies since early 2010s, mostly to celebrate IDAHOT – international day against

the civil society until the latter recognizes the former and perceives it as an active, mature, and politicized group. In other words, we will always fail in a more broad-based mobilizing the population if we continue to ignore the political relevance of the problems facing the same population and fail to recognize the forms of struggle they have chosen.

The Tkibuli strike is a conspicuous example of civil society's identification with a marginalized group and its involvement in the latter's struggle. Workers' movements have traditionally been at the core of civil activism and social movements. In the case of Georgia, the workers' extreme structural feebleness and political marginalization, coupled with the absence of labor rights, makes the workers' resistance more akin to the resistance of political society than that of civil society. This is what makes the stable support by students and other civil actors so vital for the movement. Civil rights groups, while made up of members who are themselves fragile and lacking stability, are still better equipped with resources and access to information than workers are. It is through such articulation of support and solidarity that joint involvement by civil and political societies may be reached.

With this we are seeing the fruits of years of effort to mobilize leftist groups and workers toward collective action. However, when it comes to urban space, these same groups have not even started to identify the various forms of struggle that more marginalized groups have waged. At a time when the repertoires of contentious urban politics have widened and achieved certain success and stability, the next stage in the development of their politics would be to diversify in two ways: a more daring association of urban problems with wider social and political phenomena; and the recognizing, politicizing, and valuing of existing, if not yet visible, forms of resistance. As Herbert Marcuse reminds us, today, when the right to the city is increasingly becoming an integral part of new forms of urban praxis, it is important to ask whose rights, which rights, and what kind of city we are discussing.[12]

homophobia. On May 17 in 2013 however, counter-protesters mobilized by the Georgian Orthodox church violently attacked gathered members of the LGBT community. Since then LGBT activists and allies have been either trying to occupy and mark public spaces without physical presence or have staged rallies with a high police presence. Overall however, the LGBT community has been fighting for its presence in public space. Meanwhile the Orthodox Church has also been fighting to monopolize definition of public space and to become key censor deciding what norms, performances, messages, and persons are allowed to be voices and present in public space.
12 Marcuse, P., *From critical urban theory to the right to the city*, in City, 13(2-3), 185-197, accessed April 2, 2018, www.doi.org/10.1080/13604810902982177.

The Forgotten Pioneers
Sebastian Pranz
Images by Fabian Weiss
and Sebastian Pranz

The sky over Tbilisi is as dirty as its streets and courtyards. The weather vane on the balustrade is turning impatiently, and far below it lies the city, looking like a post-Soviet snow-globe behind blue-gray veils of rain. We descend the stairs, stepping carefully around broken sheets of glass and rusty corners. At the bottom we stand in front of a heavy hatchway that leads into the interior of the tower. Teimuraz Bliadze heaves all his strength against the iron wheel that locks the hatch. Cold air that smells of brine and rust rushes out into our faces. As I lean forward to look into the depths, his left hand reaches out and grabs my arm. »What is it?« I ask. »That's the cloud,« he says and smiles. »But it's switched off, we have to save electricity.«

Back in the 1970s, you might have blamed Teimuraz for the bad weather. In those days, along with a hundred other physicists, he researched hail here in the Institute for Cloud Research. Weather manipulation seemed a promising field, and was generously funded by Moscow. The physicists had the latest measuring instruments, fired rockets into thunderstorms and had airplanes that could seed clouds. But hail stubbornly defied all scientific field work, destroying the finely-calibrated instruments and making research flights impossible. On top of that, it was a rare weather phenomenon in Georgia – which yet made it all the more dangerous for the Soviet Union's breadbasket. For that reason, the research was moved into a controlled room within the laboratory, and a tower was built in which to make hail.

Big ideas were in great demand in the post-war Soviet Union. Even though the Kremlin presented the victory over Germany as a triumph, the *Great Patriotic War*, with its 20 million Soviet dead, had shown the country's vulnerability and put it into a difficult geo-political situation. The USA's head start was especially apparent from its superior war technology: jet propulsion, rockets, radar, and of course atomic weapons. By taking political control of countries like Bulgaria, Hungary, and East Germany, the Soviets had created a belt that might protect them from conventional attacks, but offered no defence against nuclear bombs. The next war, the Kremlin knew all too well, would be decided by the better ideas. Just recently, it had been the soldiers of the Red Army who had carried the Soviet ethos into the world, now in the 50s it was up to the scientists to follow them. And today those pioneers are old women and men whose faith in the importance of their work survived the collapse of the Soviet Union. They keep working, hoping for a better pension and that the next generation of scientists will save their ideas for the future.

The inside of the weather machine has the look of a stranded nuclear submarine about it: snail-shell ventilation pipes connect the weather chamber to the outside world. There are measuring instruments with milky glass, rusty levers, open fuse panels, and among all these a noticeboard with yellowing black-and-white photos pinned to it. Most of them show hail. The days when money was poured into expensive pure research are long gone. Today the institute only carries out minor measurements for others. The pioneers of weather research still use instruments marked with Cyrillic letters. Asked why the last three governments might have lost interest in hail, the pioneers offer only an evasive answer: »Maybe there are other fields that are more important.« We leave the interior of the tower

Historical photo of the main chamber. The Cloud Chamber is 30 meters high and a real cloud can be formed inside it.

Ventilation device in the Cloud Chamber. The chamber is only used from time to time as the artifical cloud consumes a lot of energy.

through a door and enter the communal office. The researchers, who greet us with a friendly smile, are pioneers like Teimuraz, people who wanted to tame the weather. Old hands are stretched out to us in greeting, chairs are pushed in front of a dirty board. One of the old men launches unprompted into a lecture on the manipulation of hail. His English is fragmentary, consisting really only of technical terms strung together: »Thermal – under Archimedes-Force – temperature rise – condensation level. Vapor transfer into water particles.« With clipped movements, he uses vectors and numbers to draw hailstones in a storm.

Looking at the Bolsheviks' scientific agenda today, you could easily get the impression that no idea was too big for a country the size of the Soviet Union. Ideas like building a giant, nuclear-powered pump station on the Bering Strait to control the currents of the Pacific and improve the weather in the northern hemisphere. In a mad rush of feasibility and futurism, even projects like diverting Siberian rivers into the Aral Sea seemed possible. The fact that this would have required building a reservoir the size of New Zealand did not slow down the Bolsheviks' ambition. This zeal for scientific research was also making a sizeable impression on the other side of the world. President Eisenhower's strategists warned him of a new form of warfare by weather manipulation, and even 1950s New Yorkers worried about floods caused by melted polar ice caps.

»If we'd had this conversation 40 years ago, we'd all have ended up in jail,« says Rafael Tkhuvaleli, his hands protectively stroking a leather-bound book. There are black-and-white pictures of geometrical bodies stuck to the machine-printed pages, and large negatives fall out of the volume as he leafs through it. »These are holograms of projectiles, they could be rockets, for example,« says Rafael. In the 1970s, he worked together with other scientists on a program for quickly identifying objects in motion. »From Moscow I received very detailed partial commissions, but I never discovered the greater context I needed for my work. That was part of the system, of course,« says Rafael. Behind him stands a row of heavy metal shelves, in which stacks of books, rolls of paper, slip boxes and piles of densely-inscribed graph paper form an irregular pattern. The other half of the room is dominated by electronic components – a chaos of cables, reels, switches and soldering irons interspersed with open circuit boards and switching circuits. The control center of Georgian cybernetics smells faintly of my childhood train set.

The evening sun throws the latticed shadow of a giant construction framework through the window. At the moment, the only way to the Cybernetics Institute is through the labyrinth of corrugated iron fences which leads to a gray building cowering at the back of a major construction site. Of its eight stories, only the lowest are being used. A few years ago, the government did make the upper floors available for the *Internally Displaced Persons* from Abkhazia and South Ossetia, but now the block is empty again, and the few discarded fridges and camp beds seem a little out of place. We follow Rafael through darkened corridors. Every now and then we knock on a door and get invited to tea by friendly old men. The institute has a recruitment problem. The youngest cyberneticists here are in their early 50s. At some point we end up in a small office. The room has been almost completely cleared. There are torn-out pages and

index cards lying around between clipboards, cables and an abandoned gas mask, all of which are covered with a sepia-colored blanket of construction dust. »I worked here for more than 30 years until we moved downstairs,« says Rafael.

In the 1960s, Rafael was one of five young physicists to receive a scholarship in Moscow. When he was subsequently offered a job back in his home country, he was quick to leave the capital – at the time, the Cybernetics Institute was one of the leading institutes in the Soviet Union. Over a thousand scientists were researching questions here about which most of their contemporaries did not have even the remotest idea. And yet those in power showed a lot of interest, for they saw military potential in cybernetics. The top secret commissions that Rafael and his colleagues were set to work on may have come from Moscow, but they could just as easily have been found in Stanislaw Lem's notebook: a system that reads brainwave patterns in order to determine whether a tank driver is about to fall asleep; a map of the Siberian hinterland that can predict the location of diamonds based on a comparison of satellite imagery and regional folk tales. »Moscow liked our work. We were renowned scientists across the whole of the USSR,« said Rafael, and a glimmer appears in his eye.

Cybernetics was the hottest iron in the Cold War between the superpowers. The study of complex »control systems« that could be observed and steered developed into a school of thought whose post-modern charm hardly any other discipline could resist: biologists began to study the interactions between cells and their environment, psychologists propounded the idea of the human spirit as an information machine,

131

and computer scientists began to develop decentralized networks. In America, cybernetics concentrated itself around the eccentric mathematician Norbert Wiener and so found itself in the gravitational field of the legendary Massachusetts Institute of Technology. Next door to the cyberneticists at MIT, another ambitious project was being founded whose leader was an enthusiastic participant in Wiener's colloquiums: along with his research department and furnished with money from the defense ministry, the computer scientist Joseph Carl Robnett Licklider was working on a research network that could connect the supercomputers of all the different American universities. It was to be a decentralized system in which data found its own way to the nearest node, a system perfectly suited for the distribution of academic knowledge, but just as useful as a military network, because in the event of a first strike from Russia such a decentralized network would still be capable of responding. While Rafael was working in the closed system of his institute in Tbilisi on subtasks that came from Moscow via the secret mail system, his transatlantic colleagues were working on the same questions in their interdisciplinary think tanks, but beneath different political figureheads. History was to fall on the American side: ten years after the Soviets had fired the first satellites into space, the West had recovered well from its Sputnik shock. But it wasn't Neil Armstrong and Buzz Aldrin who wrote history in 1969, it was the students of America's cybernetics pioneers, who put the ARPANET online and so inaugurated the internet age.

The pattern of shadows on Rafael's desk is slowly subsumed by the glare from neon tubes. »It's really very sad that Georgian cybernetics rests on the shoulders of a few old men,« he says. For many years now, the 79-year-old has been getting by with small research projects. His salary was raised a little last year – before then, it had been difficult to pay the rent on the flat he shared with his brother. The fall of the Iron Curtain drastically changed the situation for Georgian science. In the Soviet Union, two-thirds of research was financed by the military, but this most important source of income for applied research dried up as the defense budget shrank in the 1990s. At the same time, the Soviet pioneers were suddenly trapped in a worldwide competition whose rules had been written by the West. The fact that the majority of the Soviet research results have never been translated into English has damaged international understanding – as has the fact that new and different empirical procedures have become standard in the West. But a larger chasm has opened between different ideologies: on both sides, scientific research had put itself at the service of the state. Now in the clash of new scientific systems, the Soviet pioneers were suddenly faced with the question of how the knowledge accumulated by the last two generations of scientists could continue under a different political system.

»In the West, our research results would only be valid if they got tested with the sophisticated procedures of a clinical trial,« says Inga Giorgadze. »But if you have a sick patient, there's no time for expensive experiments.« The professor runs the laboratory at the Eliava Institute of Bacteriophages in Tbilisi. She took over the job from her father, a considered pioneer of microbiology in the 1920s. Bacteriophages are highly specialized viruses that feed exclusively on bacteria. That means they

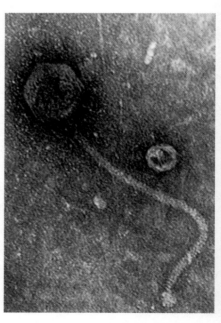

A bacteriophage is a virus that replicates within bacteria. Once the bacterium gets infected it dies, spreading more phages that attack the surrounding bacteria. Bacteriophages are thus considered to be a possible alternative for antibiotics.

can, in principle, heal any bacterial illness – from a simple gastrointestinal infection all the way up to anthrax. As a child, Inga ranged the institute's huge grounds, and rode the horses whose urine the doctors used to create serums to treat tetanus. When she cut her knee, or drank water from a dirty puddle, her father would summon her to his office and give her a glass of cloudy phage juice to drink. The story of how she successfully led the institute into privatization in the 1990s and now works together with people who could be her grandchildren is closely linked to Georgia's medical history. Her most precious capital is the more than 1,200 phage strains that have been stored in the institute's cellars for over a century like a well-cooled treasure.

It was the Georgian bacteriologist Giorgi Eliava who brought phage research to Georgia from France in the 1920s. Stalin was so taken with it that he funded an entire institute for this nascent branch of science. The next 20 years became a golden age of research in France and the USA as well as Georgia – but it was only in the USSR that phages became a real medicine for the masses. When World War II broke out, and wound infections became rampant in the field hospitals, the West switched to a new treatment that had just become market-ready: penicillin. But since manufacturing antibiotics was expensive, and certain vital patents were only registered in the West, the Soviet Union continued to treat bacterial infections mainly with phages – and with some success. And so as the war raged, Georgia became the centre for bacteriophage research – a time capsule in which Eliava's phages survived both the war and the chaos of independence decades later.

The Research of Bacteriophages started in the 1920s. Stalin was so taken with it that he funded an entire institute for this nascent branch of science.

134

Physicist Anzor Gvelesiani outlines how hail can be manipulated within a cloud.

On the table in front of me there are microscopic black-and-white photos of bacteriophages, like pictures of the young grandchildren. This new progeny is the pride of all the researchers – and they already have beautiful examples in their collection. If a standard medicine offers no cure, Giorgadze's team of researchers develops a specialized phage strain, and the refrigerated archive in the cellars grows. In fact, this hundred-year head-start could well come in useful soon, since interest in phage treatment has recently revived – not least because of the growing fear of multiresistant pathogens. When antibiotics don't help, phages could work real miracles without creating new resistances. »We had a patient from Germany here last week,« the professor says. »He had a bad wound infection on his stomach. Back in Heidelberg they were about to remove his muscle tissue, but I told him: if you do what I say you'll be well again soon.« The demand in the German market is growing, even if phage treatment is still banned there. »When we sent him home two weeks ago, our German colleagues almost lost their faith,« she says, her face creased with smiles.

»How much longer are you going to work?« I ask Inga as I'm leaving. She takes off her glasses and gives me an attentive look. »We'll see. If God gives me a little more time … you know, if you don't commit your body and soul to your work, you won't get very far.« Rafael too will keep going to his office every morning, through that labyrinth of building sites that could match the complexity of a cybernetic circuit diagram. He still has a lot of ideas. More than fit into one scientist's life. He's just presented the government with a concept for an information centre to collect the country's seismographic data. »The future of artificial intelligence is in the early recognition of natural disasters,« he says. But he was unable to get the funding because he couldn't meet the criteria that required young scientists to be involved in the research. Meanwhile the institute will soon be renovated – there are to be new offices and an information center, and Rafael is sure that some young people will come soon after. And then cybernetics will unleash its magical powers once more.

Inside the weather machine, Teimuraz talks of the cumulus clouds and their complex beauty, while outside the rain drums against the windows. The institute for cloud research is now reduced to working on small subtasks and carrying out atmospheric measurements for other institute's experiments. »Science is an expensive pleasure,« says Teimuraz. »Of course we'd like to have more opportunities, but we're happy with what we've got.« He has worked here for 30 years, and his greatest achievement is the erection of the weather chamber that is now falling apart. »Sometimes I get the feeling that we created something here that we still haven't fully understood,« he says.

4 Broadcasting the City, Broadcasting the Self

Broadcasting the City, Broadcasting the Self

Broadcasting the City, Broadcasting the Self

Broadcasting the City, Broadcasting the Self

Broadcasting the City, Broadcasting the Self

In 1995 Georgian Artist Mamuka Japharidze disguised himself as a technician
for an invented TV station, approached
the Mtatsminda TV and Radio tower,
and asked to enter. Here are selections
from his performance, taken from the
top of the tower, where the traces of civil
war are evident across the city:

*Having fastened a video camera on my
head, I climbed 200 meters up the inner
ladder on the Tbilisi communication
tower, or what remained of it after the fire.
On the platform I marked a spot with a
stencil and made video and photo shots
of the city. I remember playing the video
at the artists' display in the basement
of Republic Square the next day. For half
an hour it showed how I was walking up
the iron ladder, the steps in the dark
vertical tunnel, my tired breathing, and
the noise the wind made through the
holes in the burnt iron structure. Hard
times they were. You could even call
it anarchy. One day my studio was broken
into and I lost the tape. I still have these
photo negatives from the tower, though.
So many things have changed. This is
no longer the city we knew then.*

Mental Transformation in Post-Soviet Tbilisi
Gia Khaduri

There is this Russian slang word – *sovok* – that literally means dustpan. The term was coined at the dusk of the *perestroika* era and refers to the Soviet man of that time – or more precisely, to his standing, aspirations, mentality and outlook on life and the world. A Georgian *sovok* would obviously have been no different from any other *sovok*, but he still reflected a mentality somewhat specific to the country.

Georgia, which had the longest history of statehood among the Soviet nations, had often been at the brink of extinction due to the aggressive colonial policies of neighboring Islamic and then Soviet empires. For that reason, its people had developed a fierce sense of national identity to secure the integrity of the nation and national character. In the case of the Soviet empire, the main factor keeping Georgia in tight ideological proximity to Russia was the figure of Stalin – the ethnic Georgian who ruled the Soviet Union from 1941 until his death in 1953. When the link broke after his death and defamation, there arose a generation in Georgia in the 1960s that was totally disappointed with the socialist system. As a result, the communist ideology began to suffer a severe devaluation.

In order to eradicate the germ of protest in Georgia, the Kremlin turned to a subtle and ideologically flexible policy of governance, which proved effective in placating nascent dissent. This was especially true in Tbilisi, which was the hub of Georgia's intellectual, creative, and financial energies. The policy was such that the Kremlin built an illusory sense of freedom by not interfering with explicit expressions of pseudo-patriotic strife or free speech among poets and directors, and tried to keep its censorship away from the media. It even turned a blind eye to illegal incomes and the plundering of socialist properties. In this way, it encouraged an attitude of complacency across the entire population, which in turn aggravated certain unhealthy ambitions among the public.

This is how the phenomenon of the Soviet Tbilisian was created. It was totally different from the inhabitant of any other major Soviet city – be it a Kievan, an Alma-Atyan, or even a Moscovite. A Tbilisian did not deem himself a *sovok* and thus carried a prideful air wherever he went.

These tendencies were particularly prevalent among the youth who, starting in the 1970s, became increasingly susceptible to a so-called »street mentality.« This was not an accident, as it ideally suited the interests of Kremlin ideologists in Moscow who cynically understood that a younger generation will always need space to direct their rebellious spirit. In the West this was provided by youth culture – the space traditionally created and defended by the young. Had Georgia enjoyed even the modest degree of freedom enjoyed in the Eastern Bloc, the country would have been an ideal arena for this creative self-realization. However, we found ourselves isolated from the cultural processes under way in the West at that time, and the defining characteristics of youth culture became illegal in the USSR. As such, the heavy-handed ideology of Soviet culture has had predictably negative associations for us since childhood.

The huge gap between these two streams of culture and thought helped create an immense vacuum in the consciousness of an entire generation. This was the vacuum that was eventually filled by what we called the »thieves' ideology«, or the underworld tradition, as the only available mode of dissent and opposition to an otherwise dominant Soviet state of affairs.

This ideology of the thief reached something of a formal status during the Soviet period in the character of the *vor* – a code-bound thief that today is defined as a figure associated with organized crime. Years ago, however, the picture was much more complex. A *vor* was a lone wolf, an anti-social criminal dropout. He was bound only by the thieves' code and was not subjugated to any particular criminal organization. There was more to his criminal activity than just the accumulation of wealth, for he did not have the right to ally himself with any state institutions and did not recognize any authority.

Theoretically, a *vor* would not meddle in the everyday life of ordinary citizens and his »just« and severe laws would only apply in the criminal world. In practice, however, the influence of *vors* eventually reached all aspects of life, including the political establishment, and particularly affected young people who came to view *vors* as selfless, romantic individuals opposing the system. It goes without saying that not all people in Tbilisi shared this perspective, but they still had to reckon with the unwritten mob law fed by *vor* ideology.

Soviet ideologists, for their part, did everything to encourage this spread of criminal romanticism among Tbilisi youth. They sought to channel their rebellious spirit into a manageable course, and to prevent alliances with more politically active values such as those that guide today's youth culture. One of the ways this was done was by fighting western subcultural formations, which sprang up every now and then in Tbilisi. The system, with its official ideology, persecuted such underground movements, because they were perceived as champions of a bourgeois western culture that undermined the Soviet order.

At the same time, the various subcultures also provoked the city's layabouts caught up in the *vor* ideology. Their eccentricity, extravagance, and offbeat way of life was perceived as an indecent gesture by Tbilisians in particular and toward Georgian identity in general. The subcultural movement, as modest as it was, inspired a natural interest and intrigue among Tbilisi youth, and was regarded by those taken with the *vor* mentality to be a challenge to their grip on the ideology of the new generation. It was in these paradoxical ways that the interests and goals of the oppressive Soviet ideology overlapped with the seemingly freedom-loving street mentality. This is how jumbled the life and people of Tbilisi were, how badly they were entangled in mutually exclusive values in Soviet times.

The first serious hope for individual and societal breakthrough came with the dawn of perestroika. *Perestroika* and its associated »openness« raised big expectations among segments of the population who no longer wanted to remain *sovoks*, who were sure that weaker ideological pressure would lead to a wider stage for self-identification and self-assertion. Western European and American tourists, sociologists, and artists began to flock to the city, and regular contact with these visitors helped create new horizons in the collective consciousness. American students brought with them a new range of cultural references, and this exchange had a tremendous impact on our mentality and taste. As our understanding of the West began to transform, so did Georgian youth culture. While we gradually realized what a truly free world, a free human, might mean, we also realized that the conflict between an embedded, conservative establishment and progressive thought was no less acute in the western world.

So while we felt we had come close to some sort of truth , there proved to be more significant cultural forces that were a real mental test for Tbilisians and which would bear painful and irrevocable fruit in the future.

The weakening of ideological pressure and censorship served as a stimulus for the rise of the national liberation movement in the country, and Tbilisi's streets and squares provided the arena for its activities. Soon we witnessed large demonstrations and rallies that summoned people to defy the Soviet government and to support exit from the USSR. These summons were often based on nothing but emotional appeals and pathos. It was clear most people were not ready for what was to follow, as only a handful realized what kind of phenomena freedom and democracy were and how much it took to change the patterns that had been cemented in people's minds for 70 years.

In practice, the struggle against Soviet colonialism was not based on humanistic, liberal values; rather, it was built on narrow-minded nationalistic positions fed by archaic worldviews and conservative ethnic discourses. While I cannot claim this trend did not worry anyone, the people who were concerned about it were so few they failed to shape mainstream thought. When the philosopher Merab Mamardashvili, the »Georgian Socrates« of the 20th century, saw that the movement had taken the wrong path, he announced publicly: »Truth is a higher category than patriotism«. The public pressure that followed, including the branding of the philosopher as an opportunist, quickly led to his death from a heart attack.

The result was a new stereotype of what the »true« freedom-fighting Georgian should be, what he should think and do, and even what he should look like. Any counter-cultural or subcultural deviations, once perceived as acts of defiance against communist culture, were now thought to be anti-Georgian. For example, I remember quite well how hard it was for followers of the new Georgian alternative rock culture, who were persecuted by both official authorities as well adherents to this pseudo-national ideology for something as simple as their appearance.

The aforementioned »street mentality« had not disappeared either; it had only transformed into an accomplice to this new conservative movement. It is remarkable to think that it was the new Tbilisi rock culture of the time that revealed the flaws of the now un-romanticized »City of Sun and Roses« – a place where dominant, conservative values often overshadowed the freedoms of individuals and interfered dramatically in their daily lives.

The tragedy of April 9, 1989, when the Soviet army dispersed a rally and that left behind 20 dead, further weakened the Kremlin's influence in Georgia and strengthened the National Movement. One of its branches, led by Zviad Gamsakhurdia, even came to power in the subsequent elections. But only a year passed before Tbilisi witnessed a real civil war break out on its streets. Gamsakhurdia was deposed and the Soviet Union collapsed. Georgia, from the very first moment of its independent life, faced a destructive decade of civil and ethnic wars, bloody political confrontations, bitter poverty, soaring crime, drug addiction, and a crushed population who spent these ten years in the literal and metaphorical dark.

When a longstanding economic and political system collapses and a nation attempts to build a new one, the process is often marked by the destruction of existing structures. However, many events that followed the Soviet collapse in Georgia were also caused by the actions of the irresponsible and profiteering political elites of the times. In doing so, they sacrificed an entire generation – as young Georgians, especially those coming of age, had to bear the consequences of the ensuing situation. They are now often referred to as the »lost generation,« and this is partly true as those ten years took away the lives of numerous young people, undermined moral values, and brought the violence and vice of the city to the surface.

The city became an arena for warring gangs of armed adolescents, who lived on racketeering and no longer had anything in common with the street romanticism that had been so relevant in the Tbilisi of Soviet times. What inspired them were gangster films, not the *vor* codes that claimed fairness and justice. Is it not remarkable that their favorite film was *Once Upon A Time in the West* by Sergio Leone?! They became more violently pragmatic, oriented toward raw profit, and merciless in their tactics. The police, frightened and functionless as they were, abdicated responsibility as a semi-formal, armed militia of beardless boys patrolled the streets. And it should come as no surprise that the population feared them no less than the official police, as extreme poverty, a survival instinct, and a sense of impunity put these gangs beyond the control of any authority. It became impossible to set up any kind of business, however small, and avoid the threat of extortion that had become the norm at the time. This is why everyone was armed and all activity was regulated by mutual, often criminal agreement – not by the rule of law.

Such a situation naturally caused severe anxieties among the population; particularly on the part of the young people, who found such methods of survival totally unacceptable. Many of them ceased to see themselves or their future in the city and did everything they could to flee the country. The most tragic part was that a sizeable portion who emigrated at the time were the healthy, resourceful, and visionary youth that was capable of reviving the ideals that were now vital to post-Soviet, independent Georgia. Luckily for the country, many of the younger generation who bore such potential and managed to retain their integrity amid the dark years stayed in Georgia. They could be found everywhere – in government positions, in the non-government sector, and even in the street. It would seem they did not have any leverage to mend the disrepair, but it was they who advocated, in their respective circles, a set of common civic values without which it was impossible to even think of a bright future. Without this advocacy and struggle not only Tbilisi but the entire country would not have had any hope of survival. This was a true battle.

A battle between a possible future and its potential failure. A struggle that called for a mental transformation.

It was becoming clear that the fight was led by those representing the new Georgian counter-culture. The movement that we now call the Georgian underground of the 1990s encompassed artists, poets, writers, directors, and musicians. Notwithstanding the harsh conditions, they organized exhibitions, concerts, festivals and semi-covert alternative spaces – real oases where young people could socialize, mix and enjoy themselves. It soon turned out that the young who had been deemed outsiders and who had found it extremely hard to exist in Tbilisi, »in the whore of a city that is the realm of wolves where honesty was killed,« were quite numerous and they sought each other out. Such places included the remarkable space created by the guru of Georgian alternative music, Lado Burduli, in an abandoned silk factory; the studio and library of the conceptual artist Mamuka Japharidze; and the handful of youth clubs that kept springing up, being shut down and reappearing (such as Kazbegi, Aura, etc.). In 1995, designer and artist Gela Kuprashvili even organized an unprecedented, large-scale festival of avant-garde fashion and art that lasted a week. This project clearly showed what high standards Georgian underground culture had reached, while being subjected to political oppression, social hostility, and battlefield conditions. It was full of truly non-conformist spirits. It goes without saying that hedonism had a sizeable share in the movement, too; but it was an underground hedonism – active, affective, honest, and uncompromising – and it would periodically illuminate a city that, often without electricity for months, could be taken over by the dark.

The number of people involved in the movement was still growing. Gradually, it became apparent, even to those living a criminal life, that their spiritual or physical recovery was only going to happen by their own hands. Many were just tired of the precarious life and started to look for ways to channel their energy, skills, and ambitions positively. This was also the time when a lot of young people put down their weapons, picked up books, and started to study. Many others turned to the guitar or the artist's brush and have often found success ever since.

The most important aspect of all this is that, the reigning vice in the Georgian political elite notwithstanding, the country chose the only correct direction and started to build a European state. There was no longer any ideology that could restrict anyone. Society was open and information regarding the cultural, social, and psychological grounding of European attitudes flowed freely into the country. More and more people (though still relatively few) could now afford to travel, study, and even do business abroad. Many saw with their own eyes what constituted western political life – the ability of a society to organize itself, respect for the rule of law, the protection of humanistic ideals – and the demands this model required from each citizen. The sharing of this new vision of citizenship helped replace hopelessness and apathy with faith in the future. It was still early to call it a victorious tendency, and it is still early now, but one thing is evident: the process had become irrevocable and this was what mattered.

In the early 21st century it became evident that a new progressive section of society was making new demands for radical reforms to address the political and economic crises of the country, and draw up new vectors of development. This was a time when a large group of young, western-educated politicians, economists, and lawyers emerged who had a vision of what was needed to achieve these goals. The country, meanwhile, was still being steered by outdated profiteers whose interests did not include social change or political progress. There was a growing awareness at the heart of the Rose Revolution that such people had to be driven out of the political arena and that the country had to be shifted to a new path. And it was the support and effort of Tbilisians that steered the event to a successful outcome.

These days one hears much about both the virtues and vices brought about by the nine years of Saakashvili's regime. But one thing is never questioned: at the dawn of its rule it managed to wage an effective and successful war against the debasement that had permeated government and business structures. It turned out that it was possible to eradicate corruption and the shadow economy, and to rein in the excesses of the criminal world. Few could envision that the struggle against the street mentality, grounded as it was in decades of uncontested practice, could be so successful in such a short time. Fewer still imagined that the myth of invincibility that surrounded the *vor's* world would shatter so quickly.

However, the fiercer the struggle, the more abnormal the government's methods became. It was the leadership's greatest mistake that they tried to force progress upon the country – a process which in practice takes decades to complete. It takes people with a long-term vision to carefully structure a new state. The transformation of a collective *mentalité* is a lengthy, painful process; and for the process to be successful, policies should be flexible, well-timed, and careful. New cultural and social vectors have to be drawn alongside economic and political ones. Sadly, the young government's visions were quite rushed, and that is why they applied such brutal methods to achieve their goals. Is it surprising that Georgians, and particularly Tbilisians, took this personally? It read as an impingement of their identity, an insult to their liberal values, and a humiliation of deeply-held sensibilities. Their reaction was intense, active, and argumentative.

While it is true that the leadership in question lost its position due to the clashes that followed, the struggle for a more liberal and tolerant state would grow to an unprecedented scale in the future. This process was greatly supported and accelerated by the influence of social networks, whose role in the discovery of »new« values proved essential. The youth is at the forefront of this struggle for new values. It is they who force society and government to compromise and listen to their demands. They are not content with what has been attained so far. Today the fight is for a true liberalism as opposed to a pseudo-liberalism, a fight that includes: the protection of minority rights; a political rather than pseudo-moralistic understanding of patriotism; gender equality; and fundamental freedoms of self and group expression. This is an uncompromising, relentless fight. And it is young women and girls who stand at its frontline – whose role in social life is becoming increasingly articulate and visible. Of course,

152

there are still plenty of obstacles. But it is also true that the new generation is striving to find and invent new identities that challenge the archaic identities of the past. They also understand that they need to learn from and articulate new intellectual resources to achieve their goals.

It would be foolish to say everyone here thinks alike or that the progressive vision of this generation is the deciding vector of future development. This is certainly not so. But this is an active minority, a vigorous group who have faith in their choices – who understand that there is no way back and who look forward at all times. This is why their ranks are swelling daily, why their space is expanding, and why their effort is destined for success. I personally believe the biggest threat facing us is the longstanding »Georgian« trait of impatience. We all know that the transformation of society cannot be attained through a mechanical sharing of progressive values. It is only achievable through constant and methodical refinement of one's perception and understanding – through mental transformations. It is a long and complex path, which took the West almost a century to walk – and at a huge cost. There is no universal recipe for how one should walk the road or what it will look like. It is very individual, both on a personal and a national level. We may not yet know what the Georgian road looks like, but we do know we must follow it . The rest is just not important.

Home Altars
Fabian Weiss

Georgian identity has deep historic roots in its relationship to Christianity, with the founding of the Georgian Apostolic Autocephalous Orthodox Church in the 1st century forming a central tenet to the narratives of national identity. However, during Soviet rule, many churches in Tbilisi were closed down or converted into secular buildings. Strictly speaking religion was not forbidden, but the message was clear: visiting a church on a regular basis aroused suspicion by the officials. It was not until the last days of Soviet rule that the Church was allowed to re-open churches and consecrate new ones, in a broader process that continues to tie the Church to ongoing questions of urban investment, legal authority, and economic responsibility.

With the degradation of public religiosity during much of the 20th century, spiritual life shifted to private spaces. The primary expression of this emerging sacralization of domestic space is the home altar. Whether part of an elaborate architecture or simply occupying interstitial space, individually decorated home altars are not only a sign of personal belief but also an expression of the self. As with so much of material culture, these altars and their adjacencies map a new constellation of competing meaning, values, and aspirations. Still today one can find home altars that show the spiritual plurality of belief that has emerged within the domestic sphere in these years of transition.

155

158

163

165

Dying-into Tbilisi
Elene Margvelashvili

Lying on my back on the hard pavement of a pedestrian crosswalk in Tbilisi, I closed my eyes and smelled death. Anesthetized by the chant of the protesters and the snapping of cameras on the World Day of Remembrance for Road Traffic Victims, I had one image in my head: a guy from 10 years ago who did not survive a motorbike wreck in Boise, USA.

When I stopped at the wreck, the police were already there. There was hardly anything left of him: the pavement had eaten him. It was raining hard and he had been driving an old 1960s Harley. He had my respect, even though I never knew him. And now I never would – except as another road fatality statistic.

There, in front of the Georgian parliament, taking part in a »die-in« protest with 20 other road-safety activists, the police officers glanced over us just like they glanced over the victims: 100 dead and 4,000 injured on the roads of Tbilisi every year. Breathing some of the deadliest air on the planet, I thought of the physical death of one person and the many other ways to die in a hostile city. All of us in Tbilisi, whether we admit it or not, know that the cold grip is never really far away.

A good city is measured by the extent to which it builds identity, fosters self-esteem, and promotes positive community values. In other words, it is a place that works on a human scale – an environment oriented towards its inhabitants. By these standards, Tbilisi seems to be failing us on multiple scales.

The failure of successive governments to meet urban challenges have hollowed out public interest and deprived citizens of the right to a stake in the life of the city. An overall plan for Tbilisi hasn't been formulated now for generations. The city authorities' lack of will to envision, plan, and execute sustainable urban development is a reflection of a deep-seated apathy and prevailing public attitudes that accept the prerogatives of private interest. Lifestyle changes in the past few decades, as well as the unquestioning embrace of neo-liberal economic governance, have led to what some smart-mouthed commentators have termed »urban collapse«. To me, it feels more like my hometown is on its deathbed, showing ever fewer signs of life and vitality.

»I don't want to be in traffic from morning till night,« sings the frontman of a popular local band, Mother on Mondays. Over the past decade, poor traffic organization, courtesy of Tbilisi City Hall, and the addition of road infrastructure in a shortsighted attempt to solve congestion problems, smoothed the way for more cars in Tbilisi. Poor driving, low-levels of enforcement, and inadequate pedestrian infrastructure have left Tbilisi's streets a hazardous place to roam for anyone on foot – with a third of all car accidents involving pedestrians. Despite the fact that two-thirds of Tbilisi residents don't own a car, the fear of causing discontent among drivers by imposing severe car control measures drives the vicious cycle of car-oriented development and all-out dehumanization.

Sidewalks – once powerful symbols of the public realm – are now routinely seized by parking, construction, and private business, leaving pedestrians with few or no safe walking options. At major crossings, pedestrians are consigned to dank underpasses or steel overpasses, barely accessible by foot, let alone on wheels.

Private transport is becoming the only safe option for many, while those unable to afford such luxury are relegated to shabby seats in cramped public transport – if a seat can even be found at rush hour. Designed exclusively for the car, the city's streets have become survival zones for our most vulnerable: the elderly, children, parents with strollers, and persons with disabilities.

Beyond traffic and road safety, our most important challenges are bound up in the relationship we have with our public spaces. I took my grandfather out for a walk recently, and we had to think hard before we could choose somewhere he wanted to go. It turned out that what keeps him indoors most of all is the loss of connection with the city he has known for most of his life – a city that is stored his memories.

Tbilisi's iconic squares and public spaces tend to be the first targets for redevelopment for every government determined to improve the mistakes of the previous. With little public input and a lack of coherent planning, such efforts often lead to irreversible breaks in the chains of meaning, leisure, recreation, and experience. In short, citizens become strangers in their own land.

Even the sounds of the city are becoming hollow echoes. As the exaggerated image of Soviet-era Tbilisi's spirited community turns to the other extreme, old »city songs« of praise and friendship are replaced by lousy replicas, played at ear-splitting volume by taxi and *marshrutka* drivers on a station whose name, ironically, translates as »careless«. And speaking of volume and carelessness, in a recent television show about noise pollution in the city, the host had to start the program with a long speech defining the word »accountability« since no public officials had shown up to address the concerns of the audience. Their seats were left empty.

Although good ideas tend to surface from time to time through promising municipality statements and an infinite number of strategic documents, the leaders of this city still seem unsure of themselves and go out of their way to avoid encounters with the media and the public. While cities around the world invest in developing smart citizen engagement tools, Tbilisi residents are becoming consistently frustrated by a lack of dialogue – forced unto an unhealthy round of mutual recriminations between non-responsive first-level executives, investors, and one another.

If we can agree that it takes space to create a community and a community to create space, then Tbilisi is clearly far from success. However, an alternative to the top-down approach has emerged through civil activism in the past few years. Small groups of urban activists have taken on the responsibility of protecting the public good from political, environmental, social, and cultural harm.

By creating resistance, introducing best practices, and generating collective solutions, groups like the Guerrilla Gardeners, Tbilisi Hamkari and coalitions like Ertad have empowered communities and put urban issues at the center of the public debate. While civil society is still learning to work together, grassroots campaigns and public space interventions reveal the city's potential by bringing together those who had lost faith in the possibility of change.

One way I chose to be a part of this was to leave my job at the public broadcaster several months ago and devote myself fully to a project which might help breathe new life into an unlucky, but otherwise beautiful, Tbilisi. Four years ago I took over a non-profit organization named *Iare Pekhit* (WALK), which seeks to protect the rights of pedestrians, advocate for human-centered cities, and work to form a new kind of relationship between Tbilisi and its citizens. Our work ranges from grassroots initiatives to the high stakes of drawing up municipal and state strategies.

Since community livelihood is knit together with the opportunities of cultural engagement, one way we try to build community is through the introduction of art into public spaces. By allowing people to reimagine otherwise featureless places through artwork, we seek to invite a feeling of belonging and encourage moments of questioning the spaces beyond. Our protests are also becoming increasingly a form of performance art: activists from Iare Pekhit, complete with angel wings, recently descended on a crossing in the city center to escort pedestrians safely across the road in the absence of any traffic lights to slow oncoming traffic. There was confusion, even annoyance, but the smiles on some drivers' faces showed that offbeat humor can also be a powerful way to make simple messages hit home.

Back on the cold, hard asphalt, these thoughts weigh heavily on my mind. As another activist helps me up from the road, it occurs to me that we will have to work hard together and be creative to pull ourselves out of the patterns of unsustainable urban development. We need to retrieve lost ideals of community, the public good, equity and freedom – ideals which we have let slip in our rush towards material gain and personal comfort. We also need to be firmer in our demands from public officials, and to take the initiative wherever we see it lacking.

In short, we need to bring our city back from the brink of death, and restore it to the living entity it was always meant to be. Our symbolic »die-in«, a tribute to all those who have physically or emotionally died as victims of our inhuman urban environment, is also, as much as anything, a powerful call to resurrection.

5 Fashioning a New Body Politic

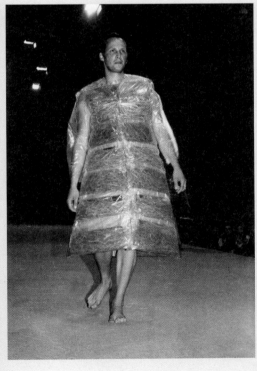

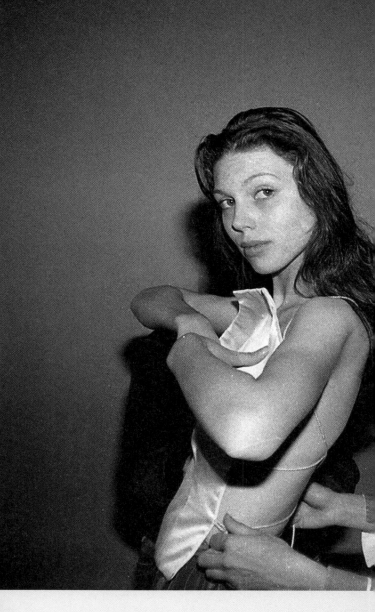

Fashioning a New Body Politic

Founded in 1995 by artist Gela Kuprashvili, the Avant-Garde Fashion Assembly (AMA) was soon to become one of the most important platforms for art in post-Soviet Georgia. With a focus on alternative and experimental fashion, it attracted artists from all fields from the Caucasus and Eastern Europe. After 1995 the festival was realized two more times – in 1996 and 1999. Coming at a punishing time in the city's history, the AMA stood as a signal moment in the years of transition following the Soviet collapse and subsequent war. It brought together an artistic sensibility that was as complex as its historical moment – with models sitting on the floor applying their own makeup in mirrors leaning against the wall, and festival-goers sitting on the wooden benches of its outdoor Expo venue.

Transformation of Urban Protests: From Spontaneous Activism to Social Movements

Esma Berikishvili
and David Sichinava

The use of urban conflict as a mobilizing factor and a tool for influencing governmental policy has a long history. As processes of urbanization accelerated in the 20th century, cities gradually, and perhaps inevitably, became places where social struggle and emancipation came together. Conflicts originating in cities are not just public responses to restructurings of the built environment; they reflect broader economic, political, and social changes underway in society. As Jacobsson points out, »Urban grassroots mobilizations arise in response to new social cleavages and increased polarization as a consequence of neoliberalization and globalization processes as well as the transformation of state power and authority.«[1]

Henri Lefebvre introduced the city as an analytical category, thus creating room for discussion on the role of urban form in changing politics. Likewise, protests taking place in such space have the capacity for great social change.[2] Broadly conceived, then, the objective of our research is to study the social and political environment of Tbilisi, which served as fertile ground for the rise of urban activism between 2007 and 2015. Through this discussion, we will also reflect on the political possibilities and controversies that are characteristic of contemporary Georgian society. This study investigates urban activist groups in Tbilisi in an effort to fill gaps in existing literature and to create a platform for further discussion on the potential of urban social movements.[3]

The new wave of urban protest movements analyzed here should be read against the backdrop of the numerous political protests of the latter decades of the 20th century, which had different agendas, atmospheres, and groups of attendees. One of the most notable historic protests in Tbilisi took place on April 14, 1978, when the city's main thoroughfare of Rustaveli Avenue witnessed the joint demonstration of Tbilisi State University students and members of the public defending the official status of the Georgian language. Throughout 1988 and 1989, the center of the city turned into an epicenter of mass rallies, culminating in the bloody massacre of protest participants by the Soviet army on April 9, 1989. The first years of independence were marred by political protests and the civil war, much of which was fought in central streets of Tbilisi. Finally, protest rallies became an integral part of early 21st-century Georgia, most vividly exemplified by the Rose Revolution of 2003, the November 7, 2007 rally, and the April 2009 *Cell Protests*.[4]

The atmosphere of these protests resembled more that of an act of civil disobedience than positive community engagement. Thus, urban protest movements in Tbilisi passed several stages of development over time. These earlier protests involved political parties contesting official government rule, whereas the later protests discussed in this paper were more focused on acute issues of heritage preservation and changes to the urban environment. These latter protests also utilized different tactics and forms of expression, such as mixing entertainment-based festivals with protesting.

In what follows, we provide a brief history of urban protest movements in Tbilisi, an analysis of the structure of protest groups, and reflections from the protesters themselves. We conclude by assessing the factors of success and failure of these protests and describe the results achieved by urban activism in Tbilisi in recent years.

1 Jacobsson, K. *Urban grassroots movements in Central and Eastern Europe.* London: Routledge, 2015.
2 Lefebvre, H. (1996)[1968]. The right to the city. *Writings on cities*
3 This work is based on the Anthology of Urban Protest project undertaken by the Heinrich Böll Foundation Southern Caucasian Regional Office. For this study we analyzed nine different protest initiative case studies.³ For a more complete portrait, we interviewed activists affiliated with Tiflis Hamkari, Safe Zone,

Green Fist, Guerilla Gardening and Green Alternative, as well as the non-aligned Gudiashvili Square rally organizers. In all, we conducted fourteen interviews. The authors would like to thank Nino Lejava, David Gogishvili, Maia Barkaia, and Suzy Harris-Brandts for their comments on the earlier draft of this paper
4 Kabachnik, Peter. »Prison, Nuisance, or Spectacle? The 2009 »Cell« Protests in Tbilisi, Georgia.« *Geopolitics* 18, no. 1 (2013): 1-23.

Setting the Scene for Urban Protests: Tbilisi and Urban Movements in an Era of Unfinished Transition Throughout the last three decades, Georgia has passed through several stages of transition in its social, economic, and political development. According to historian Stephen Jones, this transition encompassed periods of collapse, reform, stagnation, and acceleration.[5] After the collapse of the Soviet Union, state institutions deteriorated or were hollowed out, existing only formally. The resulting chaos was particularly palpable in the capital: transportation and utility infrastructure were nonexistent; informal buildings, such as garages, and apartment building extensions sprang up; and the streets turned into an arena for armed gangs. The state failed to provide even rudimentary security for its citizens. At the same time, because of the city's unclear power structures, it was often forced to reckon with a disparate range of interest groups leading to chaotic development.[6]

In the three decades since the collapse of the Soviet Union, changes to the built form of Tbilisi were generally characterized by a total rejection of planning regulations. A rapid shift to a market economy and the introduction of neoliberal reforms further resulted in dramatic physical transformations to the city. For our research respondents, the reason they decided to join protest movements in Tbilisi was to create a space to reflect upon these changes. The erosion of parks and other public spaces, and a disregard for urban heritage was for them a direct result of such transformations. In addition to any potential professional interests in urban issues or environmental concerns they may have had (for example, as architects, geographers, or urban planners), individual respondents were motivated by a discontent with existing political and economic structures directed toward erasing social activities from the city. Paramount among their concerns was the general lack of inclusivity in decision making, and many respondents said that they felt that the city should primarily function as a space for its citizens.

In the early 2000s, after the Shevardnadze government managed to consolidate power, the country initiated further reforms to transform itself into a market economy – albeit with varying degrees of success. Stabilization was hampered by the economic crisis originating in Russia in the late 1990s and was linked to widespread corruption in Georgia. Eventually, the malfunctioning political system culminated in the Rose Revolution of November 2003, which resulted in the peaceful removal of the Shevardnadze government. The protests leading up to the revolution erupted in Tbilisi after public outcry over the manipulation of the 2003 parliamentary elections. These protesters represented a broad spectrum of Georgians including party activists and average citizens expressing discontent with Shevardnadze. Led by Mikheil Saakashvili, the protesters forced Shevardnadze to resign by storming the parliament. Presidential and parliamentary elections following these events officially brought Saakashvili and his party to power in 2004.

Prior to these events, the first major urban protest in newly-independent Georgia took place when several activists and local inhabitants rallied against the mass felling of trees in Dighomi Recreational Park. During the protests, one of our respondents, artist Ana Gabriadze, went out of her way to make sure the area retained its recreational status. She

5 Jones, Stephen. *Georgia: a political history since independence.* IB Tauris, 2015.
6 Van Assche, Kristof, Joseph Salukvadze, and Martijn Duineveld. »Speed, vitality and innovation in the reinvention of Georgian planning aspects of integration and role formation.« *European Planning Studies* 20, no. 6 (2012): 999-1015.

even involved politicians, including Saakashvili, who at that time was Chair of the Tbilisi City Council. Gabriadze organized exhibitions of her own work, argued with construction workers, and finally even lay down in front of a bulldozer on the construction site. The destruction of the Dighomi Recreational Park is typical of the attitude toward urban development that existed during Shevardnadze's era. Here, development mainly relied upon the black market, corrupt bureaucrats, and their cast of shady contacts.[7] Protest actions such as those of Gabriadze were thus crucial to garnering public opposition.

The period following the Rose Revolution is particularly significant for our study due to a number of structural changes that the revolution brought about. The so-called »Georgian Economic Miracle« was based on a neo-liberal developmental model involving mass privatizations and deregulation.[8] This was a time when the central government – and to a large extent the president himself – were powerful players in various aspects of urban planning. Responding to the changes of this period, an extremely important wave of protests was initiated by the activists affiliated with the Tbilisi-based heritage preservation group, Tiflis Hamkari. In 2007 the organization had begun a series of protests against the demolition of a house at 2 Leonidze Street. But according to the organizers, this particular rally failed to attract large-scale popularity. As a result, the house was demolished. However, the protests were effective in convincing the developer to build a four-story structure instead of the initially planned seven-story one. Although the Leonidze protests failed to stop the demolition of the building, it did establish a new trend in protests in Tbilisi. These trends included exhibitions, historical city tours, and other non-violent forms of expression which were applied to social activism as a form of protest, a practice unseen before.

The same group remained at the forefront of preservation issues in the city in the following years. Tiflis Hamkari was responsible for organizing protests against the dismantling of the former Marxism and Leninism Institute (IMEL) building on Rustaveli Avenue. But the largest protest they undertook was the epic battle for the defense of Gudiashvili Square, an important historic area in the Old City. Although the initial rallies for preserving the square took place in 2007, they transformed into large-scale protests in 2011 when architectural renderings of the square's reconstruction appeared on social media.[9] That same summer, Tiflis Hamkari set up an archival photo display on the square to help raise awareness about its importance as a public space. Soon after, a larger group of activists formed to protest the transformations of the square.

Interestingly, the group aimed to arrange rallies that would look like festivals. So-called »Mini-fest as Manifesto« events were organized in the hope of attracting larger audiences. These events combined elements of entertainment, such as live music, theatrical performance, and carnival, with more serious demands for heritage preservation. Such rallies completely redefined the forms of expression in public protests that had existed for decades. These new modes of protest were also implemented in later events, becoming a popular tool of mobilization in the hands of the public. This novel form of protest established at Gudiashvili Square was also quickly taken up by other groups such as Guerilla

7 Van Assche, Kristof, Joseph Salukvadze, and Martijn Duineveld. »Speed, vitality and innovation in the reinvention of Georgian planning aspects of integration and role formation.« *European Planning Studies* 20, no. 6 (2012): 999-1015. P. 12

8 Van Assche, Kristof, Joseph Salukvadze, and Martijn Duineveld. »Speed, vitality and innovation in the reinvention of Georgian planning aspects of integration and role formation.« *European Planning Studies* 20, no. 6 (2012): 999-1015; Lazarus, Joel.

»Neo-Liberal State Building and Western »Democracy Promotion:« the Case of Georgia.« In *7th Pan European Conference on International Relations.* 2010; Van Assche, Kristof, Joseph Salukvadze, and Martijn Duineveld. »Speed, vitality and innovation in the reinvention of Georgian planning aspects of integration and role formation.« *European Planning Studies* 20, no. 6 (2012): 999-1015.

9 Zechner und Zechner Gmbh. 2011. »Gudiashvili Square Redevelopment.« December 16, 2011.

Gardening, an activist group founded in 2013 concerned with greening under-utilized spaces in Tbilisi.

In addition to the struggle to preserve the heritage of the city, protests against environmental issues were common during this period. For example, in 2010 when the government announced its plans to construct a new highway in the Vere Gorge, online activists created the »Save Mziuri« Facebook group. This page promoted protest against the loss of vegetation in the park and its adjacent river gorge and aimed to protect the area from potential developers.

In 2012 the country witnessed parliamentary elections. It was hoped that the changing government would bring about a new era in heritage and environmental preservation. In the buildup to elections, the opposition Georgian Dream coalition readily expressed its sensitivity to cultural heritage and urban development.[10] Unfortunately, after the elections the public saw no significant change in investors' or the government's approach to urban spaces. Environmental activists particularly stepped up their effort, rallying for the preservation of a park at 10 Asatiani Street in 2013 and later for the preservation of the so-called »Squirrels Area« on a slope adjacent to Turtle Lake.

In 2014 news spread that a private investor was planning to build a hotel in Vake Park and the members of Guerilla Gardening started to mobilize to prevent the construction. The Vake Park rally was a combination of several elements. Participants camped out in tents for eight months in order to obstruct any attempt at construction activities. The Vake Park protests also utilized the Gudiashvili Square model outlined above, with concerts and performances being used to garner greater public support. As of 2018, the project continues to be suspended, as the Guerilla Gardeners have gone to court to have the construction permit annulled.

In 2015, the Georgian Dream government announced two large-scale reconstruction projects in Old Tbilisi which threatened existing public space. The Mirza-Shafi Street reconstruction and the Panorama Tbilisi project instigated another wave of protest as citizens considered such actions to be a continuation of the same unilateral approach to urban development employed by the previous government. Following the presentation of these two projects, a protest movement organizing under the name *No to Panorama*, represented the first time in the city's history that saw several protest groups coming together in solidarity to resist top-down development. This is how what has come to be known as the *Together Movement* was born. The *No to Panorama* movement involved both street rallies and judicial components. On the one hand, the movement organized protest rallies against the development while also relying heavily on courts to address the dispute.

Protesters, the Arena of Protests, and Party Politics In studying the structure of these protest groups, we found that the majority were not formally established organizations and had no clear leader, with each member having equal rights. Many of our respondents noted that they did not view the formalization of their movement as a necessity, preferring instead a model of participation with an open framework. For example, as Mariam Bakradze, a Guerilla Gardener, said: »Guerilla Gardening is an ordinary civic organi-

www.worldarchitecturenews.com/?fuseaction=wa-nappln.projectview&upload_id=18360.
10 Bidzina Ivanishvili – Georgian Dream Electoral Bloc – Electoral program, www.ivote.ge/images/doc/pdfs/ocnebis%20saarchevno%20programa.pdf [seen: 20,02.2016]

180

zation, whose main value and attraction lies in it being a *movement*, not an *organization*: it being a live, ongoing process.« Similarly, recruitment into the Guerilla Gardeners followed an open membership approach, where interested participants were not subjected to any particular qualifying procedures. This model of participation extended to funding structures, with the majority of groups being funded through voluntary member contributions. On the one hand, self-funding and enthusiasm-based activism ensured that urban protest groups were freer in their action planning and execution. On the other, however, if more secure sources of funding were available, these groups may have had more access to the resources needed to better mobilize people to take part in their protests.

Even though the urban activism scene in Tbilisi encompasses several groups, the methods they use to plan and organize rallies share certain key approaches. For example, the use of social networks to mobilize members and disseminate information is a common practice. The activists mostly communicated via Facebook, which proved to be a useful tool in recruitment and in the discussion and decision-making processes. Actions were mainly planned in closed Facebook groups where a consensus was reached by various methods. There are, however, notable exceptions. Members of the *Green Fist* movement abandoned Facebook as a platform to make important decisions because they preferred in-person meetings to discuss various issues, including planning rallies. Green Fist member Khatia Maghlaperidze stated: »Face-to-face meetings are important; however much you may post on Facebook, meetings are still necessary. Once every few days, or even every day during times of crisis, we will meet and talk about what needs to be done. The Tbilisi State University garden is usually the place.«

In most of the activist groups studied, members did not explicitly engage with official party politics, but still saw their actions as political. For these activists, involvement in popular protest was a crucial expression of citizenship. Urban activists try hard to maintain distance from partisan politics because they were worried about being manipulated by politicians. For example, Manana Kochladze stated: »When politicians show up … they start to manipulate.« However, as her colleague Mariam Bakradze reiterated, anything urban activists undertake is indeed political: »Everything that surrounds us, everything that is happening is certainly politics.« Another protester, Nika Davitashvili of Guerilla Gardening, claimed: »It is not only what happens in parliament, with the government administration, in the city council, or city hall … there is much more politics in what ordinary citizens do.«

There are several actions that have prevented party politics from creeping into the city's protests and rallies. For example, activist groups have avoided the use of overt political symbols, including party slogans and flags, and have instead requested that politicians participate solely as citizens. That said, the disagreement about the coexistence of social and political components within the same protest was a key factor inhibiting the consolidation of the city's various protest movements. Conflict within the *Together Movement* in 2015 is a good example. The movement organized a rally against the Panorama Tbilisi project on January 31, 2015, where all the groups participating were represented by their respective insignia: Guerilla Gardeners were wearing green caps, while Green Fist brought red and green flags. The rally attracted a large crowd and was very impressive and quite noisy. As it ended, however, it became evident that the groups involved disagreed about a number of issues, such as the degree to which political opinions should be expressed at a rally. In line with this, red flags used by Green Fist were perceived as a deal breaker, as they were too affiliated with the group's political stances. Some participants thought such paraphernalia gave the rallies an unacceptable political shading. As the disagreement deepened, the Together Movement disbanded.

Notwithstanding our respondents' lack of official political involvement, some emphasized that anyone actively engaged with the cause should ensure that political demands are made. For instance, Tiflis Hamkari activists Alexandre Elisashvili and Tamar Amashukeli expressed the need to shift urban topics into mainstream political discourse. Moreover, Elisashvili eventually ran as an independent candidate in the 2017 Tbilisi mayoral election and was able to finish second after government-endorsed candidate Kakha Kaladze.

Reflections of Protesters   Our interviewees' assessments varied when they spoke of the results that the movement had brought about. Their ambivalent attitudes could be explained by their differing expectations about what the protests were supposed to accomplish. The respondents discussed both extremes extensively: the shortcomings of their groups' activities and their most positive and memorable experiences. For the majority of our informants, these included the Gudiashvili Square protests, the *No to Panorama* movement, and the Vake Park rallies.

The main indicator of success described by most respondents was the temporary suspension of the opposed projects. Interestingly, other respondents deemed this outcome as one of the demonstrations' failures since there was no guarantee against future development. Reflecting the former position, Nika Loladze of Guerilla Gardening stated: »If we consider both rallies (Gudiashvili Square and Vake Park) successful, then success will lie in freezing the problem, not resolving it.« Expressing a more ambivalent position, Tamar Gurchiani claimed: »If we measure success by the fact that Gudiashvili Square is not a Chanel boutique store now, then yes, we were successful. But, they still managed to turn the area into a hell.«

Another positive outcome the respondents named was informing the public more broadly and raising awareness of urban issues. Up until the Gudiashvili rallies, almost all the protests had either been directed at state-level problems or had taken place with each group defending the rights of their own. As a result, respondents felt that today the number, geography, and interests of those involved in urban protest movements are much larger than before. More people are getting to know about the various local hotspots in Tbilisi, which has had a very tangible result. Being more informed also diminished the citizens' sense of indifference. Just based on the Vake Park movement alone, many people concluded that their voice mattered and that there was a point to them taking to the streets.

Concluding Remarks   Over the course of the past three decades, activism in Tbilisi has shifted from political critique to more focused concerns related to the built environment. Describing urban social movements more broadly, Della Porta and Diani claim that informal contacts based on shared beliefs and solidarity on the one hand, and conflicts that will unite people and groups on the other, are crucial components to effective urban social movements.[11] The empirical data we collected corroborates such claims. We found that informal contacts play a significant role in the lives of urban groups, helping the activists to solve their problems. While Tbilisi's urban social movements have been effective on many fronts, the range of issues addressed by the protesters remain limited, including only those of urban heritage, cultural and historical identity, and the environment. Economic inequality, the right to decent housing, and homelessness, often remained outside the focus of Georgian urban protesters.[12]

The groups in Tbilisi used different resistance tactics – noisy rallies, performances, and legal struggles – and were generally characterized by the specific features pointed out by Manuel Castells: their protests were related to the city; and they were limited by and based in a particular urban area.[13] Apart from these features, group identity, ideological position, and organized collective demands play a significant role for urban social movements,[14] and this was as well evidenced in the case of Tbilisi.

In the course of analyzing the origins of urban social movements in Tbilisi, we became aware of the role that the social and political environment has played in their development. According to sociologist Sidney Tarrow, people generally engage in contentious politics when new opportunities for resistance emerge.[15] The changes that began during the latter stage of Shevardnadze's regime and led to the Rose Revolution could be seen as one such opportunity for urban protests in Tbilisi. Indeed, the Rose Revolution brought about major changes, but establishing effective public protest in its aftermath was also challenging. For example, while Tiflis Hamkari stepped up its activities in 2006, its efforts still remained spontaneous and lacked mass popularity. The political rallies of November 2007 and their well-shaped organization overshadowed other, less prominent, forms of urban activism taking place at the same time.

When the Georgian Dream coalition attempted to introduce urban issues in its political agenda prior to the parliamentary elections of 2012, these issues began to receive greater attention, which also created a new opportunity for resistance. As the activists themselves reflected, under the new government politicians appeared to hear their concerns but fell short of implementing actual changes, whereas under the previous government their voices were hardly heard at all.

Urban social movements in Tbilisi are now being presented with an opportunity to shift towards conventional party politics, an arena that could gain them more mainstream popularity. Entry into party politics by some activists, such as Elisashvili or Amashukeli, suggests that the urban agenda will soon take up a significant portion of Georgia's political discourse and that spontaneous activism will gradually turn into a more structured social movement strongly grounded in its urban roots. For those concerned with these issues, this points towards a more promising future.

11 Della Porta, D. and Diani, M., eds., *The Oxford handbook of social movements* (Oxford University Press, 2015).
12 The only exception was the initiative suggested by Urban Reactor and entitled »House for All« in which the activists reacted to the eviction of refugees from various buildings.
13 Castells, M., *The city and the grassroots: a cross-cultural theory of urban social movements.* No. 7. (Univ of California Press, 1983), 328.
14 Tilly, C., *Regimes and repertoires* (University of Chicago Press, 2010), 185.
15 Tarrow, S. G., *Power in movement: Social movements and contentious politics* (Cambridge University Press, 2011), 29.

Market Imperatives
Text by Sarah Cowles
Images by Fabian Weiss

Eliava

Hot faucet flip, piezo count 1-2-3-4-1-2-3 spark Kaztransgas flame,
inline coils heat water, gone squat boilers idly hoarding heat.
      – shit, sorry darlings –
singe *tsamtsami*[1]: the girls troubleshoot cheap heater's burnt stink,
heater's plastic parts heat, disintegrate, incinerate, *gapuchda*.[2]
      – *Vaime, modi tsavidet eliavaze*[3]. –
      – Eliava – I am afraid – we must go to Eliava –
Eliava: *chacha*[4] shot bolts gut sigh. Eliava, ground metal, oiled soil, Astra[5]
smoke, *»marto xar*[6]*«*? Ply the woven warrens of Eliava, on Mtkvari's
left bank, seek tankless 7 liter-perminute grey market *tsqlis gatboba*.[7]

      Market Eliava: born black, gone gray. 1990s Soviet disunion,
microraion[8] construction halted, material's inertia rerouted, URAL [9]
flatbeds bank surplus, parked Left Bank Mtkvari, Stacked Kruzchev
precast panels effect shifts tectonic: was wall, was enclosure, now
bridge, now roof.

      Aside Bagrationi Bridge abutment, hammer drills hole, set drill,
lean blue duffel coat men, market's-labor-market. Labor: *remont*[10]
Gldanis microraion *binebi*[11], block and tackle, debris down, blocks up,
block in the balcony. Labor: fitting out Didi Dighomi's[12] *tetri karkasi*[13]:
draw conduits, run pipes, splice, interlock laminate PVC straps.

      Eliava: proto-hypermarket: flooring, fixtures, cables, carburetors,
lighting, laminates, drills, grills, grindstones and hoses, housewares
and housings.

      Eliava: signs read the 90s divide: industrial cognates Russian,
digital cognates English.

      Amortizatorebi[14]:shock absorber, hold, release energy, *fleshka*[15]:
flash card, accept, hold, release information. Eliava: information
exchange: expertise + parts + gossip. Know-how, Know who-who.

1 *Tsamtsami*: Eyelash. Tsami: One second, tsamtsami, the time of the blink of an eye.
2 *Gapuchda*: It's broken.
3 *Tsavidet eliavaze*: Let's go to Eliava.
4 *Chacha*: A potent Georgian home-brewed spirit,
distilled from grape skins.
5 *Astra*: A brand of unfiltered inexpensive cigarettes.
6 *Marto xar*: Are you alone/single?
7 *Tsqlis gatboba*: Water heater.
8 *Microraion*: A planned urban microdistict, usually
outside the city center. Soviet-planned community.
9 *URAL*: A brand of Russian heavy-duty service
trucks used for construction, extraction and lumbering.
10 *Remont*: Remodeled apartment.
11 *Binebi*: Apartments.
12 *Didi Dighomi*: A microdistrict on the plains of
western edge of Tbilisi, known for high winds and
speculative developments. Construction of Didi
Dighomi was halted after Georgian independence;
many towers remain unfinished.

Drone picture of Eliava Market.

Internal Displacement

     – Minsk![16] –
Igori points to the refrigerator-
     Igori says we never did *remont*, in Soviet times, never bought
new, no, we banked everything, interest accumulated. Then came
the 1990s; shock, devaluation, inflation, conflicts and conflagration.
Now better to remont, too risky to bank.
     Idled Minsk stores pots and pans: new LG cools food.

Panning the Abkhazia coast, near Ochamchire:
     – *moitsa..aha..chemi sopeli*[17] –
     – Where are the roofs, Igori *bidza*?[18] –
     – *Omi*[19] –
Igori: polite on my ignorance. Igori: then farmer, now miner. Kochara[20]
cleansed, heat displaced from humid subtropical tea and citrus, to
Borjomi's geothermal strata, sulphur exhale, spruce pollen clouds,
alpine temperate: *kargi haeri*[21].

Igori makes remont, *bavshebi*[22] on one floor, *tineijerebi*[23] above,
displaced 3 units left.
     – *meshvidze, tu sheidzleba*[24] –
     Ten tetri liftis mafiastvis[25] coin box clink coins
     Borjomis Xeoba[26]: parallel Kaztransgas conduits line façade,
heat decentralized, sidelined santorium façade, block in balcony,
house generators.

13 *Tetri karkasi*: Literally, white carcass. Contemporary flats are sold unfinished, without fixtures. Individual purchasers complete construction as time and budget allow.
14 *Amortizatorebi*: Shock absorbers. Literally: amortizers.
15 *Fleshka*: Flash card.
16 *DayZ*, a multiplayer online survival game about a post-catastrophic-virus, zombie-dominated world, features a Minsk refrigerator is a bounty, described as a »power hungry household appliance to prevent your ketchup and sad vegetables from ageing.« (sic)

17 *Moitsa, chemi sopeli*: Wait, here is my village.
18 *Bidza*: Uncle.
19 *Omi*: War. The Abkhaz-Georgian war of 1992–1993. Both Georgian and Abkhaz forces inflicted civilian casualties and attempted ethnic cleansing. Georgian nationals that fled Abkhazia found refuge in abandoned civic buildings throughout Georgia, and some reside in permanent camps. Borjomi, with its many abandoned sanatoria, is home to a significant population of *internally displaced persons*, or IDPs.

Calling Water

      – Tsqali ar aris.[27] –
      – Tsqaroze tcavidet?[28] –
Water's out. Climb Mtatsminda's trail, source fills Likani bottles.
Springs: memory, faces, names and dates carved: life voiced from
tapped earth.
      – lamazo, saqvaerlo, sixarulo[29] –
The vocative case personifies a quality, it calls, it evokes.
Add -o- to the root. In the poem »Anduquaparo« Machavariani poem calls
to Saqartvelo's rivers, evoking a union of east and west, reuniting
Abkhazian and Georgian, and associates them with the great Georgian
poet Galaktion Tabidze.
      – bzipo
       enguro
       alanzano
       mtkvaro
       iaro[30]
       ager axlaxans gardatsvlilo galaktiono[31]
Tbilisi plays the dys-place in Partisan film. Gather cables in Vere ravine,
tap into the grid, build utopia. *Izloenta*[32] urbanism squat power
splice, green and yellow stripes PVC ubiquitous, insulate and join
frantic forces.

      2015 hard summer rain; Tsqneti ravine slides clogs Vere, clog
dam fails catastrophic. Instantaneous geological time, floods' scour
displace homes, roads, lives.

      Tigers loosed in Heroes' square.

      Vere meets Mtkvari, Mtkvari east to Caspian Sea. Kvirila: shout-
ing river, slate with manganese ore. Kvirila greets Rioni in Zestaponi,
flows west to Black Sea.

      Hoarded energy hoards danger: better to open that flow, tap in,
divert, transform.

20 Kochara: an ethnic Georgian village in Abkhazia on the Tskhenistskali (horses') river, now depopulated.
21 *Kargi haeri*: Good air. Borjomi's alpine climate and air currents are considered restorative for many pulmonary illnesses.
22 *Bavshvebi*: Children.
23 *Tineijerebi*: Teenagers.
24 *Meshvidze, tu sheidzleba*: »seventh floor please«.
25 *Ten tetri liftis mafiastvis*: ten tetri (cents) for the lift mafia. Communal services, such as elevators in post-Soviet Georgia, are often controlled and serviced by neighborhood »mafias« who collect service fees. Elevators are usually 10 tetri for the first 10 floors, an additional 10 for anything beyond.
26 *Borjomis Xeoba*: Bojomi Gorge. A former health resort, Borjomis Xeoba is now occupied by refugees from the Abkhaz war, who have converted the hotel rooms to apartments.
27 *Tsqali ar aris*: There is no water. Water service interruptions are common in Tbilisi.

Drone picture of Samgori Market.

Drone picture of Eliava Market.

East West split displaced in Tbilisi. East at Navtlugi. West gathers at Didube, Didube Metro, Okriba Avtobus terminal; Oqro: gold, stored value. A heat exchanger to the west: Imereti, Samegrelo, Guria, Adjara.

Marshrutkas[33] idle between vendors, speakers blare Khevsurian fanduri. Storefronts fortify the market's edge: veterinary + apiary implements and Monsanto seeds.

The Georgian genitive case, formed by adding an -s to the root, is not unlike the English apostrophe's possessive. Yet the genitive denotes more than possession: it binds nouns to their origin; it embeds generations.

The genitive brokers concrete relationships, where adjectives truck in the abstract: *Goris vashli, sachkeres sulguni,samegrelos xurma, borjomis tapli. kobuletis mandarini*[34]

The subterfuge of parts of speech: the genitive modifies like an adjective; it possesses the noun and does the adjective's work; while the adjective, *zedsartavi saxeli*[35] merely hitches a ride.

Stand on the kiosked island, breath cigarette shaurma and diesel atmosphere. Borjomi's mashrutka idles.

– ara, ar sheidzleba … sirxvili[36] –

He possesses me, but here it is shameful to kiss him goodbye.

28 *Modi, tsavidet tsqaroze*: let's go to the spring.
29 *Lamazo*: You, beauty; you, favorite; you, happiness. One can »call« a quality of someone or something by adding the vocative ending to an adjective. This use often implies a relationship – or a desired relationship-between the one calling and the subject.
30 *Bzipo* …: Poet Mukhran Machavariani lists the major rivers of Georgia in the vocative case.
31 *Ager axlaxans gardatsvlilo galaktiono*: The recently deceased Galaktion Tabidze.

32 *Izolenta*: Green and yellow striped electrical insulating tape. Russian portmanteau of »*elektroizolyatsionnaya lenta*«.
33 *Marshrutka*: Fixed route taxi, usually a multi-passenger van. The most economical public transportation system in Georgia; private marshrutka networks provide shuttle services between major cities and rural villages.
34 Gori's apples, Sachkere's sulguni, Samegrelo's persimmons, Borjomi's honey, Kobuleti's mandarin oranges.

Drone picture of Didube Bus Station.

Navtlughi

Samgoris metrosken[37] is the farm market Navtlughi: a manifold to
Kakheti's vineyards, Gurjani's orchards, and Tusheti's alpine pastures.
The instrumental case denotes is the means by which you
do something: add – it to the root.
    – Mashrutkit an taxit momiqvan?[38] *–*
Smells of sardapi – cellars – milk and udder skin, onion roots and
bruised herbs.
    – aba, gasinje[39] *–*
Navtlugi: a spread of energy storage technologies: dried, pickled,
fermented, Churkhela strings in shades of ojaleshi, saperavi, rkatsiteli
pelamushi, binds walnuts and hazelnuts.
    Sweet grape scent gradient to sour *dzmari*[40], pink cauliflower,
green cabbage in deep white buckets. Tables of stacked white rounds
of *sulguni* and *imeruli*; mottled blue stones of *dambal xacho*[41], Ford
Transit van piled high with thickets of *tsotsxebi*[42] bristles. *Tsotsxebi*:
onomatopoetic sound of sweeping.
    – chkuit, sayvarelo, chkuit chemo kargo[43] *–*

En Route to Paris, Via Beijing

George Guledani

The simplest way to catch a glimpse of the Dirsi Housing Estate is to take a drive on the Tbilisi-Rustavi highway. As you leave Tbilisi, and right before you reach Factory 31, you will see a cascade of white rectangles rising from the brown foam of industrial artifacts and rusty landscapes. Floating above the gray rails along the river, it rises like a white mirage flowering up on the far bank – a slightly dangerous, mysterious, and faraway land, of a size found nowhere else in our city.

Google Maps would advise you to get there through an alley that starts at 53 Bogdan Khmelnitsky Street. When you get there, though, you will find a suspiciously narrow road. If you have already seen the scale of this minitown from the other side of the river, you will know immediately that this cannot be *the* road to Dirsi. A woman in the tobacco kiosk advises you which way to go: »Go forward. There's a petrol station right after the traffic lights. You'll see a neon sign. The street goes in from there – a lit street.« This must be closer to reality. We turn the corner at the sign and, judging from the fact that all the traffic signs have turned their back on us, take the exit into the estate.

While Dirsi is a white mirage in daylight, it rises as a more definite shape at night. Cutting a distinctly un-Tbilisi silhouette, the scale of the entire estate, along with its particular building forms, are strange for a person born and raised in Tbilisi – be it Gldani, Varketili, or any other suburb. This creates a certain distance from the Georgian context. If not for the small ruins and Soviet-style blocks beyond the estate's perimeter, or the ubiquitous TV Tower shining down from the hill in the distance, you might think you are in a millionaire district in St. Petersburg, Dubai, or even China. In Dirsi, we don't see the results of creative projects undertaken by dwellers settled three months before – such as iron bars welded to hang the laundry or the walled-off balconies that mark the rest of the city.

Unlike other new settlements in our city, Dirsi is quite orderly – with the roads, parking, pavement, and bike paths all properly painted. The whole area is very green. Each block is equipped with a sign lit with the house number, under which stands a glass chamber with a concierge, day or night. The »mini-town« has a large playground with beautiful pirate ships. There's also a promenade along the river with a view over the Tbilisi-Rustavi highway, looking back over the Mtkvari at the whispering cars going by.

If we compare Dirsi to its Georgian counterparts of similar scale (e.g. the former Akadem-town behind the Sports Palace), we may see it as a step forward. But if we put it side by side with the post-modern Noisy-le-Grand in Paris, which of these places would one choose to live in?

Large ex-Soviet cities in Russia and Ukraine, as well as developing countries in Asia, produce entire conveyor-belt products of paradoxically exclusive and standard concrete quarters – with their own kindergartens, hospitals, playgrounds, and bike paths. When crime levels in these cities finally diminish, these housing complexes will gradually fill with dwellers. The future of such estates are generally defined by the trajectory and political stance a specific country takes. Some of them will be brought down and bulldozed flat, as has happened in many European and American cities. Others will remain orderly and controlled, just as they do in authoritarian, free economies of the Middle East and Asia. And some will turn into caricatures of isolated oases, as has happened in the suburbs of Kiev and St. Petersburg.

Nobody knows where the Dirsi »mini-town« will end up. However, in today's global economy, the complex is a logical statement of Georgian urban development – demonstrating that Tbilisi is being transformed into a regional megalopolis built around Chinese, Arab, and other international investments.

Contemporary urban health research describes such settlements in quite negative terms. These low-quality dwellings ignore the form and scale of traditional human coexistence, and estrange people from each other. Much research has confirmed that such massive-scale dwellings – with their huge spaces, microscopic personal shells, and artificial public zones – will ultimately have negative emotional effects on their dwellers. However, demand for such »mini-towns« still persists in many contemporary cities. Such mega-quarters may also be characteristic of transitioning and developing economies, where investment and the amassing of personal wealth is a temporary priority when compared to a sustainable cultivation and regulation of the urban environment.

The desire of the masses to stay close to economic centers often neglects the psychological factor. Existence in the architectural matrix is a given for many. There are even people who take the forest of gigantic blocks of flats in the middle of a bare field as the inspiration for a dystopian, romantic style, as a direct and pure expression of modern society.

6 Representing the Republic

Representing the Republic

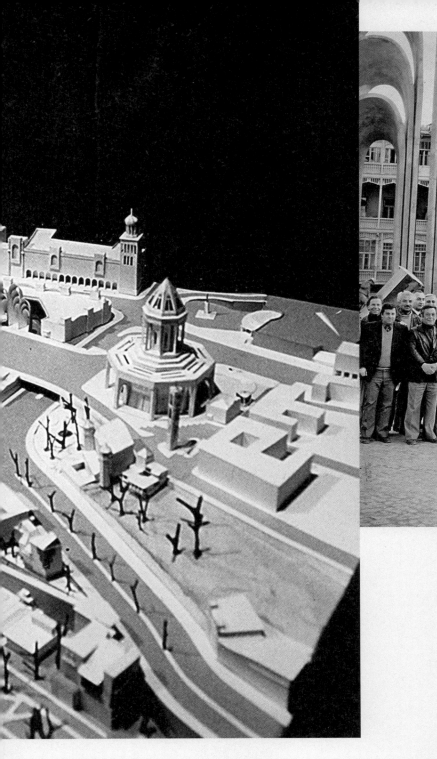

Representing the Republic

No single space in Tbilisi charts the changing contours of political vision, social aspiration, and public investment as clearly as Republic Square. Now known as Rose Revolution Square, this space emerged as central to both the transportation map of the city as well as the representational aims of various political regimes. Designed by one of Georgia's most significant post-war architects, Otar Kalandarishvili, the square includes the Iveria hotel tower, the seven-lobed podium archway, and a multistory public space and multiuse structure. The promise of the Square remains that of an urban terrace – overlooking the Mtkvari River with the Tbilisi hills as a backdrop. The following images are from the private archive of Otar Kalandarishvili – and include sections, elevations, models, and photographs. As with so many building projects from the Soviet era, many aspects of Republic Square have been destroyed and rebuilt with a new vision for the city in mind.

Out of Place[1]
Tinatin Gurgenidze
and Sebastian Weber

Georgia's fluctuating politics have always been reflected in Tbilisi's Republic Square: a space that has moved from being a military parade ground to a sanitized commercial space, playing host to Soviet relics and a vertical refugee camp along the way. And while the square is geographically the same, a lot has changed. The place is not only one of Tbilisi's few public spaces, it is also arguably the place where political and social transformation are most deeply reflected in urban and architectural space. Here, the recent past and precarious present are visibly mixing, creating an absurd, underutilized space in the heart of town.

Now named the Rose Revolution Square (after Georgia's Rose Revolution of 2003) the site still occupies an important place in the cultural imagination of the city despite having undergone significant changes over the past decades. In 1995, on a sunny 26th of May, Georgian Air Force planes created a spectacle for a crowd that had gathered for Independence Day. When it was still called Republic Square, the square had already found itself the setting for a military parade four years earlier, albeit this time in celebration of Georgia's independence shortly after the collapse of the Soviet Union. However, the air still contained the distinct scent of war on that day in 1995, as the square was the epicenter of a tragic civil war waged in the capital from 1991 to 1992. As a silent reminder of the recent conflicts, right in front of the audience stood the run-down Hotel Iveria, which was now home to over 800 Abkhazian refugees.

The story of this square goes back to the 1960s, when Soviet Georgia was one of the top tourist destinations in the USSR. In 1967, the construction of the tallest building in Tbilisi was finished: the Hotel Iveria, a 22-story structure designed by the Georgian architect Otar Kalandarishvili in the geographic center of Tbilisi and visible from every point of the city. Yet despite its visibility, this prestigious hotel was clearly not accessible to everyone. In order to book a room one had to make a reservation several months in advance through the official travel agency of the Soviet Union, *Intourist*. Only the luckiest were able to stay in one of the rooms with a great view overlooking the entire town.

Along with the hotel, Kalandarishvili also designed the square in front of it, which was finished much later in 1983. The square was built like an urban balcony on steep terrain, and was to offer a wide-open view of the river to anyone – just like the one you might enjoy from one of the exclusive rooms in the Hotel Iveria. As the architect himself described it at the time: »In the center of the city, one of Tbilisi's most important squares will be established by leveling an existing dip in the terrain. The space created underneath the square will contain more than 20 thousand square meters of useful space on three levels that will be used to create a social cultural center«. The architect wanted to create an open space and a new central square in Tbilisi, a space dedicated to popular public gatherings. One long side of the square was designed with an elevated podium, standing tall with seven arches – the so-called ›Andropov's Ears‹ (named after Yuri Andropov, General Sectretary of the Communist Party of the Soviet Union) – while across from this podium the square expanded into the horizon, overlooking the city and the Mtkvari River.

In 1992 the former Hotel Iveria became home to hundreds of refugee families from Abkhazia. Once a fancy hotel in the heart of the city, it

Aerial picture of Hotel Iveria from 1988.

1 This article was previously published online on www.failedarchitecture.com

206

The Rustaveli Arches were the most prominent feature of Republic Square. They where torn down in 2005 when the then-new president, Mikheil Saakashvili, promised to renovate the whole area around Hotel Iveria.

was now turned into a vertical refugee camp. Many of the war's *Internally Displaced Persons* settled here, looking for a temporary place to live – a situation that lasted for more than a decade. During that time, the temporary residents of the hotel changed its architecture to create a livable space – giving the building its distinct, piecemeal look from the outside. On the inside it was very packed, dark and dense, as someone who visited the place in 1997 explained. He also mentioned that it was considered a dangerous place to go, and visitors would not stick around longer than necessary. The hotel remained a dark spot in the consciousness of the city, and served as a highly visible reminder of the country's recent problems and its tumultuous present.

After the Rose Revolution in 2003 the new government became increasingly concerned with the ongoing informal construction in the city. The new president, Mikheil Saakashvili, called for the hotel to be emptied of its inhabitants and restored to its original condition as soon as possible. In 2004 the internationally successful Silk Road Group (who had owned the hotel and adjacent square since 1994) began moving out its inhabitants and started a huge restoration project. Only the skeleton was left from its original structure – and what was once considered an important monument of the city had lost its distinct look, yet again. The refugees living in the hotel were only given two months to move out and to find another place to live, together with $7,000 per room for compensation.

The Silk Road Group hired the Berlin/LA/Beijing-based architectural firm GRAFT to transform the building into a 5-star hotel, which was

Draft by architect Otar Kalandarishvili.

opened in October 2009 in grandiose fashion. Predictably, GRAFT described the redesigned hotel as a new landmark and beacon of optimism for the future of Georgia. The new government also promised to renovate the grounds around Hotel Iveria, including Republic Square. Once again, reconstruction of the Square took slightly longer and started two years after the opening of the hotel. The Portuguese/Georgian architectural studio NOA was put in charge of the project, and was also commissioned to design a commercial, multifunctional building on the square which, ironically, was to be built on exactly the same site as the previous podium from which one could watch the military parades.

Perhaps unsurprisingly, given its significance within the city, different governments have renamed and redesigned the square to articulate their newly-acquired power. And as these political powers change, already existing monuments on Rose Revolution Square keep disappearing and reappearing with a new look. In 2005 the newly elected Saakashvili government ordered the destruction of the seven arches of Andropov's Ears that had become a symbol of Georgian communism, and which had a reputation as the most hideous Soviet monument in Tbilisi. Noticing that these arches were just one example of a much longer list of slated demolitions, Tbilisi's architectural and cultural circles made the square a central topic of debate around city building and preservation. Today, a large number of architects and cultural figures are fighting against the construction of a cable car station on Rose Revolution Square that would connect the center of Tbilisi to Mtatsminda Park – a large amusement park on top of Mtatsminda Mountain. With a station placed in the middle of the square, it would once again change its look and also the face of Rustaveli Avenue, the city's main boulevard.

After independence and a destructive civil war, Georgia was quick to erase as many traces of the Soviet past as possible – and the Rose Revolution Square was not spared. Today's new government is again changing the space, recently removing yet another monument and opening the Iveria Café. So, ironically, by trying to change the situation, history continues to repeat itself. In a constant state of mutation, various episodes and histories of the square overlap in the memory of Tbilisians, preventing the place from being integrated as a stable and functional public space in the city.

Indeed, as we can see, Rose Revolution Square has long been a showcase of political ambitions. But while the square remains a physical space in Tbilisi, it is simply not used as a living place by the greater public. Most of the surface area is still reserved for cars and the huge area underneath the square has become a menacing space occupied by small businesses, offices, strip clubs, and brothels. Perhaps the one thing that has not changed across its history, and that will probably stay the same into the future, is that while façades, monuments, buildings, and even names are easily altered, the people of Tbilisi will follow their very own individual logic to integrate the square into their everyday lifes.

Degradation of Public Spaces

Surab Bakradse

With time, the degradation of public spaces in Tbilisi has become more apparent – with streets, squares, and parks falling so far in quality that they significantly lag behind any modern standard. Poor organization and neglect of public spaces, along with their domination by vehicles, has resulted in the further degradation of social life in our streets, squares, and parks.

Public space is designed and managed for social uses, so in identifying this problem we are faced with the question of whether the present condition is in fact a reflection of broader social decline. The question is entirely legitimate, as public space is the preeminent city system created for public activities and, when transformed into a three-dimensional space, stands as a visual icon of a city's values around public life. Thoughts about this issue should prompt us to look back to the Soviet era.

Alongside the deterioration of personal initiative, the primary and most severe consequence to emerge after the end of the Soviet era is the discrediting of all that is related to social or public matters. The false notions of social belonging, the constant promotion of brotherhood and equality while the opposite was demonstrated by the actual regime, cost these ideals their credence. These deficiencies were masked by the Soviet regime via ideological violence, and no sooner was the basis of violence – the Soviet state – removed than the deficiencies unveiled themselves with full power: limitless egoism replaced individualism while a cartel mentality took the place of social conscience. A fundamental lack of understanding of social values caused public space to be neglected, and with this came a loss of the sense of its civic role and significance. Society became a multitude of individuated entities, while public spaces turned into places deprived of essence.

As a result it should not be surprising that social distortions accompanying the transition were reflected in the fabric of the city. Tbilisi has become an icon of antisocial impulses. The hypertrophy of these impulses was exacerbated by the complete unpreparedness of society for the transformation of the 1990s. The mental legacy of the totalitarian state showed itself in a variety of new authoritarianisms: decades of longing for private ownership and the market economy resulted in industrial neoliberalism, while newly regained religious freedoms gave birth to Christian Orthodox fundamentalism. These antisocial impulses – authoritarianism, industrial neoliberalism, and Orthodox Christian fundamentalism – were clearly reflected in public spaces, an essential mirror of the whole city.

Neglect of public opinion in the arena of urban planning represents an essential part of authoritarian style of rule. Nearly all instances of willful action by authorities were met with critical reaction from active parts of the public; however, those in power are only concerned about the response to the degree that it threatens their position. There are no effective legislative and executive tools to ensure citizens' involvement in urban development. This violates the fundamental right of the citizen to manage the ownership and use of city spaces. These conditions exacerbate the subconscious attitude towards public spaces – as inherited from the Soviet legacy and supported by the transformational processes – and the lack of responsibility determined thereupon. Citizens are not granted the possibility to develop their social skills in this area.

Georgian urban development law is modeled on the German type. In theory, this model is compatible with a form of urban development that provides not only for the lawful pursuit of a market economy but also for a type based on values of the social state. This model of urban development law should have ensured, at least to some degree, a more or less socially healthy city growth in which the system of public spaces are protected from private expansion. However, this is not the case. The authoritarian style of the country's government has enabled changes to the law, clearing the way for the domination of private interest in public spaces and thus disrupting active social life within them.

It comes as no surprise then that the all-encompassing process of privatization in Tbilisi has affected public spaces as much as the state-owned means of production, institutions, and city building seen in the Soviet past. The process of sale included not only parks, recreational areas, and forest preserves, but also portions of streets and squares and even areas of the Mtkvari River. The public has been stripped of the right to benefit from territories that had been under its possession and management for decades, and which bear significant symbolic essence as well as grant a sense of identity to the city. It could be argued that this process has gradually amounted to what is effectively a seizure of public goods.

This process is notable not only in terms of changes made to the legal status of public spaces but also the fact that, in many cases, spaces in communal ownership are affected by private use – through forms of development that are incompatible with public interest and which cause spatial segregation (i.e. elimination of low-income residents from certain districts through economic pressures). Chardin Street and its adjacent public spaces can be seen as a clear example, with expensive cafes, restaurants, shops and other commercialized interests clearly now powerful enough to deny space for other more affordable uses. In these cases, the city government – motivated by increases in projected tax revenue, protectionism, or simply antisocial ideology – supports private initiatives that are oriented toward maximizing profits rather than a healthy social life.

Nearly all instances of this skewing of urban development law are the result of attempts to fulfill the interests of investors in construction projects and to maximize one-time profit from real estate. »Investor« has, in our society, become a term denoting a special privilege; even though experience shows that, due to the short-term nature of single-cycle construction, building investment is the most irresponsible type of financing. It does not require long-term planning and thus is not concerned with long-term negative effects. In this light, while investments might feature positive initial economic effects, the long term perspective of urban quality is undermined through the deterioration and thus devaluation of urban space. As this issue is not hidden from view or even particularly difficult to notice, it begs the question: Are authorities at all concerned with the devaluation of the city?

Naturally, these conditions would result in a waning demand for city planning as an instrument in the city's healthy development. In line with this reasoning, we can see the consequences for a city that is developing without planning – which is the case with Tbilisi. It has become common practice to issue construction permits for individual projects without preliminary urban development planning of the land adjacent to the site. The fundamental essence of urban planning – to plan a city according to public needs and to create legal terms for private initiatives to balance social interests – is forgotten. Such planning would ensure both the positive development of public space as well as the fulfillment of private interest. However, this has been excluded from post-Soviet urban development policy instruments, thus shifting focus to the architectural planning of individual building projects. Left without public-interest-based urban planning, granting building permits has become a crass instrument to facilitating the selfish desires of private capital, leaving architecture without its social essence. Subsequently, architects have become »servants« and »facilitators« of the self-centered aims of commissioners, with their awareness limited to private land areas and deaf to the needs of public space.

Perhaps the most egregious example of this is the occupation of recreational public spaces by the church. Construction projects in recreational spaces are much more »profitable« for the investor than building on private land, as the latter involves the demolition or reconstruction of property as well as providing alternative housing to original residents, while the former are »without owner.« Trees in these parks do not demand »shares«, and the practice of receiving construction permits by revoking the recreational status of these spaces is simply business as usual. This is the pattern that has accelerated the recent pace of elimination of recreational areas in the city.

Among the most active agents behind this process is the Christian Orthodox church. The unassailable status of private investors in our society, compounded by the undisputed authority of the church, means the latter enjoys all the necessary conditions for privatizing public spaces and building monasteries in them. Seen from the perspective of government, such close cooperation with the religious authorities has the added benefit of cementing their own power. This privilege is successfully leveraged by the church, which undertakes building in public parks while destroying vegetation and attaching a Christian Orthodox fundamentalist nature to the public space in them. It replaces the basic values of city life – respect for personal liberties, equality, and solidarity – with intolerance, obedience, and dogmatic morals.

The path to improving public spaces lies in increasing the social awareness of citizens. On their behalf, properly planned and attractive public spaces create a desire for social relationships, for exchange of thoughts, emotions and everyday experiences, and thus contributes to strengthening the sense of society. It is clear that the form – public space – and essence – the sense of social belonging among citizens – mutually reinforce each other. A double responsibility can be observed: on the part of citizens to self-organize to improve their public space and to keep pressure on the city government to maintain and develop it, and on the part of city government to develop healthy public spaces and to serve its citizens by inviting participation in urban development dialogue.

Lost River
Interview with city-planner
Merab Bolqvadze
by Klaus Neuburg,
Sebastian Pranz and
Wato Tsereteli

Tbilisi-based architect Merab Bolqvadze recently won a competition to develop a new land-use plan for Tbilisi. Instead of extending the city's boundaries, as has been the case throughout the 20th century, his masterplan seeks to reuse large areas of underutilized brownfield and post-industrial land within the existing borders. Central to the plan's philosophy is an understanding that the future of the city lies in the potential of its natural landscape – in preserving the mountains that surround Tbilisi and in bringing the river back to its citizens.

Greetings Mr. Bolqvadze. It took us 40 minutes longer to get here because of the heavy traffic in the city. What would be your approach to solving this problem?

The only possible solution that I see is developing a functional system of public transportation. This would somewhat regulate the traffic in the city. The problem is that the citizens have lost their trust in public transit, they have to be convinced that buses take them to their destination in time and are a safe way to commute. At present, buses are stuck in traffic jams like any other road user. They need a separate lane on the streets to make sense.

We have been visiting Tbilisi since 2013 and can see the many changes in that time. In your opinion, what is the most radical change that the city has undergone in the last 5–10 years?

Unfortunately, the most noticeable changes have been for the worse. There is a general deterioration in living conditions due to patterns of over-population. Also, public space is increasingly degraded as green areas – like parks or recreation grounds – are privatized and turned into building sites. Tbilisi today might have the lowest global percentage of green space per citizen – 4 to 5 square meters in comparison to the European standard of 15 to 18. Although many areas are irreversibly lost, we should think seriously about preserving, protecting, and developing green spaces in our city.

It has always surprised us that the Mtkvari River is so cut off from the city. People today cannot get close to the river because it is hemmed in by main roads.

This is indeed a tragic aspect of the development of the city: the citizens have lost their river. In fact, we have not only lost the Mtkvari but all the secondary rivers within the city as many smaller streams have been relocated or now run through tunnels under the city. Luckily there are two riverbank areas that are not yet obstructed by roads and could be preserved for recreational or landscape purposes. Any future city plan should be

213

N

214

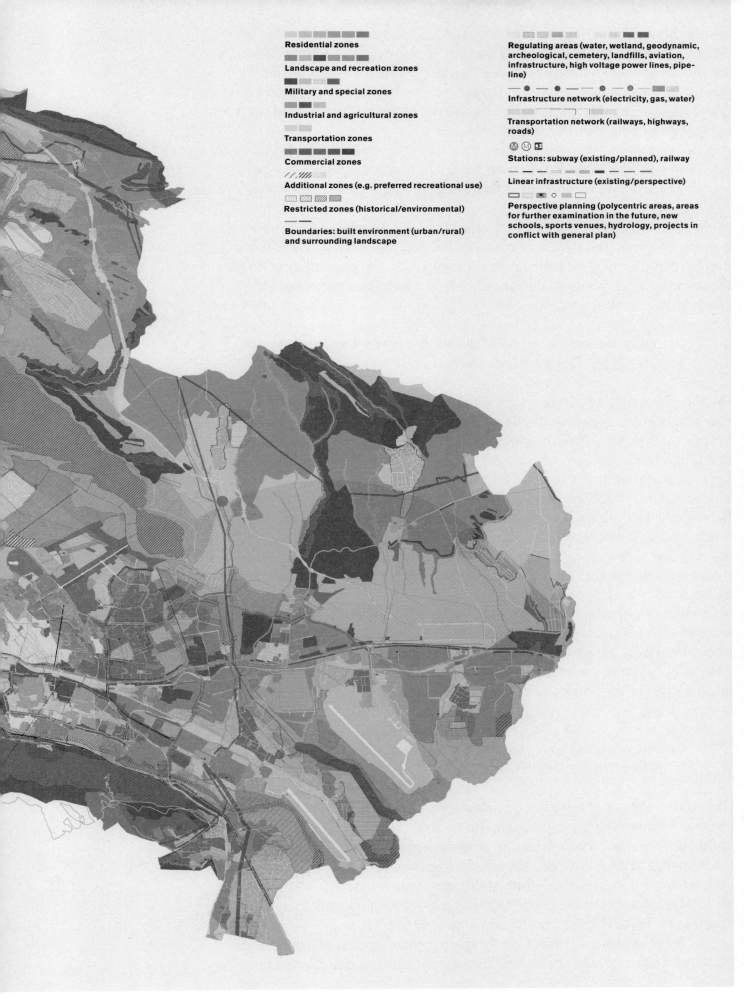

Residential zones

Landscape and recreation zones

Military and special zones

Industrial and agricultural zones

Transportation zones

Commercial zones

Additional zones (e.g. preferred recreational use)

Restricted zones (historical/environmental)

Boundaries: built environment (urban/rural) and surrounding landscape

Regulating areas (water, wetland, geodynamic, archeological, cemetery, landfills, aviation, infrastructure, high voltage power lines, pipeline)

Infrastructure network (electricity, gas, water)

Transportation network (railways, highways, roads)

Stations: subway (existing/planned), railway

Linear infrastructure (existing/perspective)

Perspective planning (polycentric areas, areas for further examination in the future, new schools, sports venues, hydrology, projects in conflict with general plan)

Merab Bolqvadze's new land-use plan for Tbilisi aims to reconvert areas of wasteland and save the city's natural landscape.
The measures are to be implemented in two stages, once they have been approved by the city's administration and accepted by the citizens.

215

directed toward opening up the many lost little rivers and streams. In addition to protecting the rivers and gorges, I think we must also focus on the mountains that surround the city. These mountains in fact define the form of the city center, so we need to protect them from being turned into crass real estate. We have chased nature out of the city; now we should at least attempt to invite it back.

In addition to the rivers, there are the hot sulphur springs that gave Tbilisi its name. How could these natural resources be used today?

As you know, Tbilisi is built atop an abundance of thermal waters. While there are currently no concrete plans for utilizing these resources, I think there are many ideas that are worth exploring – like the possibility of how those waters can be used therapeutically, for example. At present they are only used for bathing.

You have been working on a future city plan for the last few years. What is to be done to improve living conditions in Tbilisi?

Previous city plans have predominantly focused on extending the city. Our plan aims to preserve the city's existing boundaries. As a prototypical post-Soviet city, Tbilisi has large areas of wasteland with demolished or dilapidated buildings – about 850 acres by our count. The city is like a big tissue with many holes in it. This brownfield land is one reason for the city's fragmentation and lack of density and solidity. However, these brownfield territories have access to irrigation and sewage systems, and there is electricity and roads – they basically have all the resources that are needed to reintegrate them into an inhabited and productive part of the city. These territories could, for example, be reconverted into areas of ecologically-conscious industrial usage or revitalized tracts of re-naturalized environments. Measures like this would increase employment or create new recreational areas. But first of all it would give the city an attractive surface, a pleasing mosaic that re-stitches many of these urban holes. There are various projects in this direction that have already been approved, such as a proposal to construct three city parks that is currently in progress.

In what ways will your plan affect the quality of life in suburban districts like Nutsubidze or Gldani?

The central aspect of our plan is to develop a polycentric model that will remove some of the pressure from the central part of the city. We have identified five areas that will be part of this polycentric city. There are several aspects to be considered in positioning these centers: they should include a considerable number of citizens (more than 40,000); they should be adjacent to the city's major arterial roads; they should be near metro stations; and they should be multifunctional.

An essential part of city planning is to create spaces of similar economic and demographic potential. These polycentric areas are near and around Didi Dighomi, Saburtalo, Samgori, and the large shopping center

216

of East Point. We are also planning to have multiple, smaller sub-centers in the districts that would support the aforementioned polycentric areas.

In sum, the central aspects of the new urban plan include: the densification of the existing urban fabric; preserving green spaces and developing public landscapes; advocating for a polycentric model of development; a conceptual vision of reusing brownfield lands; and a sharp improvement in transportation and traffic management.

Did other urban models inspire you for your own vision of Tbilisi?

Of course there were some inspiring examples. Let us take the case of Bilbao where the river was reintegrated into the city, which has allowed a considerable increase in green areas and recreational spaces. A similar case of reintegrating the river was realized in Seoul.

What is your sense of the opinion of the population? Do people here welcome your ideas on Tbilisi or are they still skeptical?

The Tbilisi population is definitely most eager and supportive when it comes to expanding recreational and green spaces in the city. Talking about public transportation … it gets more complicated – as Georgians in general are very focused on their cars and are not aware of the effect that private transport has on our city. But I firmly believe they would consider using public transport if it was properly managed. There is no other way to solve this problem than convincing Tbilisians to use the bus.

To what extent are citizens themselves involved in forming a comprehensive plan for the future city?

I have to admit that participatory planning is a relatively new concept for us. But by considering many promising examples by our European colleagues we are working in that direction. Recently, we have had a couple dozen meetings with citizens. For instance, we have arranged a meeting with residents from Samgori and have also been approached by businessmen from the very same district. Beyond that, we have met residents from villages that have recently been incorporated into the city's territory. I believe we have covered almost all of the city's districts. Apart from some notorious worriers, we have heard opinions that should absolutely be considered. For example, it became clear that the people living in rural areas that are being integrated into the city have serious problems accessing medical care. There should be at least one easily accessed center for medical care in each of these areas. Also, many of these districts do not have sport centers and some lack kindergartens. We track all the complaints and hand the list to the municipal authorities of the city.

Who is part of the committee that approves the masterplan of the city?

Legally, the plan is commissioned by the municipality of Tbilisi. Three experts form the jury through which the plan must be assessed. We then go through their remarks and feedback and include them in our plan – or else we have to prove why we cannot include some of them. Then the municipality hands our document to an assembly that is opened for public discussion. About nine or ten such discussions have already taken place – including discussions with several ministries, universities, and scientific academies. An exhibition is also planned along with these public discussions.

> *City planning clearly requires longer time spans than one election period. Is there a risk that a new government would abandon your ideas?*

To tell you the truth, the conceptual layout of our plan doesn't leave a shred of doubt that what we propose is crucial and should be protected. The city belongs to the people, not to the political parties.

Contributors

Surab Bakradse
studied architecture and city planning at the Polytechnical Institute in Tbilisi. From 1976 he worked at the communal institute for planning *Tbilkalakproekti* in Tbilisi and studied architecture and sculpture at the Alanus University of Applied Sciences in Alfter, Germany (1994–1998). From 1999 he worked in several architect's offices in Germany as an architect, city planner, and freelance architect. From 2013 he worked as a freelance appraiser for city planning and urban planning legislation in Tbilisi. Since 2016 he has been head of the REALLABOR association that dedicates its work to the future of city planning in Tbilisi.

Esma Berikishvili
graduated with a Masters degree from the Central European University (Budapest, Hungary), Department of Sociology and Social Anthropology in 2009. Currently she is a PhD candidate at Ilia State University Interdisciplinary Program in Social and Humanitarian Sciences (Tbilisi, Georgia). Her interests and academic work include subcultures, social and urban movements, semiotics, urban transformation, and social, cultural, and visual anthropology in Georgia. In addition, Esma is an emerging producer of documentary films.

Merab Bolqvadze
received his doctoral degree in Architecture and is a visiting professor of Architecture at the Georgian Technical University. His work focuses on large city planning efforts and transportation nodes, as well as the development of general plans and development regulations for cities and settlements. He worked as chief architect and division head at Tbilkalakproekti, where his work won numerous national and international awards. Merab lives with his family in Tbilisi.

Sarah Cowles'
exhibitions and critical essays center on the aesthetics and meaning of the rudera: the systems and species adapted to disturbance. This work highlights the role of surplus materials and energy in the metamorphosis of meaning of gardens and landscapes. At the Ohio State University, she co-organized THIS IS A TEST, an international symposium on the role of testing and prototyping in contemporary landscape architecture practice. She is Associate Professor of Practice at the University of Southern California and is the 2018–2019 Kashkul artist-in-residence at the American University in Iraq, Sulaymaniyah. She has held visiting positions at Washington University and was a Fulbright Scholar in Georgia. Sarah received her MLA from Harvard University's Graduate School of Design and her BFA from the California College of the Arts.

David Gogishvili
received his doctoral degree in Urban Studies and Regional Science at Italy's Gran Sasso Science Institute in 2017. He also studied Human Geography at Tbilisi State University and Urban and Regional Planning at Stockholm University. Outside of academia, David has been involved in various NGOs and urban social movements working on open data initiatives, open source geographic information, and various issues related to urban development in Georgia and the South Caucasus. He is a founder of the Soviet Past Research Laboratory and of Iare Pekhit (Walk), both based in Georgia.

Tinatin Gurgenidze
lives and works in Berlin. She studied architecture and urban design in Tbilisi and Barcelona. Currently she is working on her PhD thesis on the (post-) Soviet mass housing settlement Gldani located in Tbilisi. Tinatin's work concentrates on the sociological approach to architecture and urban space. In her work she tries to understand what has happened with Gldani in the transition period after Georgia became independent of the Soviet Union. In addition to authoring several publications and lectures, Tinatin is co-founder of Tbilisi Architecture Biennial, which is planned to take place for the first time in 2018.

George Guledani
is a writer and TV producer born and raised in Tbilisi and educated in the States. He has worked as a producer at every major Georgian television channel and has engaged in a number of interesting writing, editing and publishing projects, primarily through magazines. In 2005 he founded Global Darkness Publishing, which has recently been printing a micro-journal, Avtopilot (avtopiloti. blogspot.com). Currently, George is editor of a newly established culture and lifestyle website, at.ge.

Suzanne Harris-Brandts
is a doctoral candidate in Urban Studies and Planning at the Massachusetts Institute of Technology (MIT) in the United States. Her work examines the politics of architecture and urbanism during periods of state building and political unrest particularly across the South Caucasus. Prior to her doctoral studies, Suzy studied architecture and is a licensed architect in Canada. She has worked at numerous design and research practices across the globe, including Toronto, Vancouver, London, the West Bank and Abu Dhabi.

Mamuka Japharidze
is an artist living and working in Tbilisi and London, who has worked on conceptual projects since 1987. His work was presented at the 48th Venice Biennial, Art in General in New York, as well as numerous exhibitions at the Georgian National Museum. Mamuka's work changes according to context and environment, and includes happenings, collections, projections, photography, games, drawings, sound design, prints, and archival work.

Levan Kalandarishvili's
38 years of experience include architectural work at various design institutions as well as participation in infrastructure programs financed by the World Bank, EBRD, and the Millennium Challenge Corporation. Recently his interests are concentrated on issues of heritage and civil activities, working with the NGOs Tbilisi Hamqari and DOCOMOMO – Georgia. He has co-authored, with Nano Zazanashvil, the brochure *Industrial Heritage of Georgia, Chiatura-Zestafoni-Poti Industrial Circuit* which reviews capitalistic relationships and architecture in Georgia in the late 19th century. Levan's collaboration with David Avalishvili and Nikoloz Mchedlidze won an architectural competition for the design of a multifunctional building in old Tbilisi, and he prepared the housing concept with architects David Avalishvili and Giorgi Margishvili in collaboration with Heinrich Böll Foundation South Caucasus Regional Office.

Gia Khaduri
is a Tbilisi-based journalist and music critic. He's been a host of »Unknown Music« – a TV program on national television for six years and an active commentator on culture and the arts in Georgia. As a journalist he collaborates with almost every important Georgian magazine, newspaper, and online media, covering a range of subjects from music and sports to socio-cultural topics.

Matthias Klingenberg
was head of the Regional Office of the German Adult Education Association (DVV International) in Tbilisi from 2012 to 2017. He is now Bread for the World's Regional Representative to the Pacific. In 2017 Berlin-based Vergangenheitsverlag published his book *Ein kleines Leben. Eine Spurensuche* (A Small Life. A Quest for Traces). At present Matthias lives in Madang, Papua New Guinea.

Ben Knight
is a freelance journalist, filmmaker, and play translator in Berlin. He writes mainly in English, but can also do it in German. His feature articles have covered weapons manufacturing in the Black Forest, Scientology in Berlin, zoophilia in Essen, pagan cults in Brandenburg, illegal fishing in Sierra Leone, Oktoberfest in Palestine, Stalin statues in Georgia, and other things up to and including colonic irrigation.

Elene Margvelashvili
is a cultural entrepreneur and urban activist from Tbilisi. In 2013 she founded Parachute Film, an audiovisual production company, where she is a producer. She was director of Iare Pekhit from 2012 to 2017 and has worked as a television host at Georgian Public Broadcasting on the daily program »Communicator.« She received an MA in Design and Visual Communication from Tbilisi State Academy of Arts and a BA in Business Administration from the Georgian-American University. She is currently studying Creative and Cultural Entrepreneurship at Goldsmiths University of London where she is a Chevening Scholar.

Klaus Neuburg
is a trained architect and works as a designer in the field of information and interaction design. His work focuses on the conception and development of media with a specific attention to spacial contexts and social interrelationships. He is co-founder of FROH! Magazine and the non-profit organization FROH! e.V., and is a substitute professor of Conception and Design at the Hamm-Lippstadt University of Applied Sciences.

Meghan O'Neill
received her Bachelor of Fine Arts from Ontario College of Art and Design (OCADU) in 2012. She has collaborated with many artists in Toronto as a performance artist and musician. Meghan lived in Tbilisi for two years and was an intern at the International Council on Monuments and Sites (ICOMOS) in Georgia for several months. Influenced by her time with ICOMOS Georgia and their Betlemi Quarter Revitalization Project (BQRP), Meghan began a Masters degree in Art History with a focus on cultural heritage preservation.

Sebastian Pranz
is a journalist and publisher living in Cologne, Germany. With a PhD in Sociology, he is especially interested in narratives of social change. Sebastian develops transmedia projects for international organizations, he is co-founder and director of the journalistic non-profit organization FROH!, and a substitute professor for digital journalism at the Darmstadt University of Applied Sciences.

Lela Rekhviashvili
is a post-doctoral researcher at Leibniz Institute for Regional Geography, Leipzig. Her research interests include the political economy of transition, informal economic practices, social movements, everyday resistance, and urban mobility. Her academic publications discuss post-Soviet shared taxis, comparing them to ride-sharing and other forms of informal transport, and the impact of institutional change, particularly of marketization policies on informal economic practices, and the role of everyday resistance in the production of public space.

David Sichinava
is a human geographer from Tbilisi. He works as a senior policy analyst at CRRC-Georgia, a Tbilisi-based think tank, and is an Assistant Professor at Tbilisi State University. Dr. Sichinava studies electoral behavior and the issues of power and inequality in urban areas. In 2016, David was a Fulbright visiting scholar at the University of Colorado Boulder. He has published on elections and urban issues in Eurasian Geography and Economics (2018), Studia Regionalia (2013), Interdisciplinary Studies on Central and Eastern Europe (2012), and on the Washington Post's »Monkey Cage« blog (2016).

Aleksi Soselia
is a curator and artist based in Tbilisi. He is co-founder of the first online archive for Georgian video art, which currently includes over 400 artworks by more than 90 artists, ranging from the 1980s until today. Aleksi currently works at the Center of Contemporary Art in Tbilisi.

Kakha Tolordava
is a TV and radio host and author at Georgian's Public Broadcast agency. From 1984 to 2000 he was a member of the Screenwriters' Board with Georgia Film, where he contributed to a number of film projects. In addition to working as creative director with the advertising agency Gudauri Studio, and working with the Institute for War and Peace Reporting, he was also Head of Communications with the World Wildlife Fund Caucasus Office. Kakha has a degree in English Language and Literature from Tbilisi State University.

Wato Tsereteli
is an artist, curator, and creative administrator. He studied Film in Tbilisi and obtained an MA from the Department of Photography at the Royal Academy of Fine Arts in Antwerp (Belgium). In 2010 he established the Center of Contemporary Art Tbilisi – an institution that occupies abandoned places in the city and transforms them into zones of urban creativity. In 2012, Wato initiated the Tbilisi Triennial – a long-term project focused on education and research into self-organized and independent art practices worldwide. Wato's artistic works are two, three, and four-dimensional

objects with well-structured spatial organizations, such as his video essay »Descriptions: Tbilisi« which was included in the 53rd Venice Biennale as part of the Georgian Pavilion, while his larger initiatives recreate public and private spaces in artistic and social settings.

Nato Tsintsabadze
is a conservation architect who graduated from Tbilisi State Academy of Arts in 1987 and obtained her MA degree in Post-War Recovery Studies at the University of York, UK. Through participation in the International Center for the Study of the preservation and Restoration of Cultural Property in 2003 she developed her specialization in Urban and Cultural Landscape Conservation. Currently she works as a program coordinator for ICOMOS Georgia and is lecturer in the Department of Conservation at Tbilisi State Academy of Arts. Nato's articles on the challenges to conservation of Tbilisi Urban Heritage have been published in Georgian and international publications, and she is author and co-author of several publications.

Jesse Vogler
is an artist and architect whose work sits at the intersection of landscape, politics, and performance. His writing and projects address the entanglements between landscape and law, and take on themes of work, property, expertise, and perfectibility. In addition to his writing, art, and design practice, Jesse is a land surveyor, co-director of the Institute of Marking and Measuring, and assistant professor at Washington University where he teaches across landscape, architecture, art, and urbanism. He was a 2016 Fulbright Scholar in Georgia and is the inaugural head of the new Architecture Program at the Free University of Tbilisi.

Sebastian Patrick Weber
studied Sociology, Urbanism and Urban Design in Osnabrück, Weimar, and Shanghai. For his thesis, elaborating points of intersection between built environment and society, he put a focus on the comparative analysis of public spaces. He works as an editor for the website competitionline.com in Berlin.

Fabian Weiss
is a photographer, visual storyteller, and member of the journalistic non-profit organization FROH! and the photo agency LAIF. His personal projects explore cultural changes in personal structures, and the cinematic images he creates are acutely observed portraits within a broader assessment of the surrounding culture and have been awarded and exhibited internationally. In addition, Fabian teaches, leads international exchange projects, and conducts workshops on visual storytelling and magazine production.

Picture Credits

Front cover (from left to right):
Sebastian Pranz/Archive of Transition
Mamuka Japharidze
National Archives of Georgia
National Archives of Georgia

Back cover (from left to right):
National Archives of Georgia
National Archives of Georgia

2-3
Sebastian Pranz/Archive of Transition
4-5
Sebastian Pranz/Archive of Transition
6-7
National Archives of Georgia
8-9
National Archives of Georgia
10-11
Fabian Weiss/Archive of Transition
12-13
National Archives of Georgia
14-15
Fabian Weiss/Archive of Transition
16-17
Gio Sumbadze
18-19
Gio Sumbadze
20-21
National Archives of Georgia
22-23
Sebastian Pranz/Archive of Transition
24-25
Nukri Jioshvili
26-27
Fabian Weiss/Archive of Transition
28-29
Fabian Weiss/Archive of Transition
36
Wikimedia
37
Visualization of Panorama Tbilisi/
youtube.com
38
Wikimedia
40-41
Rusudan Mepisashvili and Vakhtang
Tsintsadze Memorial Archive
42, 43
National Archives of Georgia
44, 46
Icomos Georgia

52-58
Rusudan Mepisashvili and Vakhtang
Tsintsadze Memorial Archive
67, 69
Matthias Klingenberg
74-83
National Archives of Georgia
85
Google Earth
86
National Archives of Georgia
87
Fabian Weiss/Archive of Transition
88-89
National Archives of Georgia
90, 91, 92
Private archive Levan Kalandarishvili
95
National Archives of Georgia
96, 98, 99, 100
Suzanne Harris-Brandts/David
Gogishvili
103
Givi Kikvadze/National Archives
of Georgia
104-105
I. Makarenko/National Archives
of Georgia
107 a
Ivan Shlamov/National Archives
of Georgia
107 b
National Archives of Georgia
108 a,b
Viktor Morgunov/National Archives
of Georgia
109
National Archives of Georgia
110
Felix Krimski/National Archives
of Georgia
111
Otar Turkia/National Archives of Georgia
112 a
Givi Kikvadze/National Archives of
Georgia
112 b
National Archives of Georgia
113
Anatoli Rukhadze, Givi Kikvadze/
National Archives of Georgia
115
Hualing promotion video
116
Aleksi Soselia/Archive of Transition
117
Aleksi Soselia/Archive of Transition
119
Aleksi Soselia/Archive of Transition
120-121
Jesse Vogler/Archive of Transition
128
Personal archive Cloud Chamber
129
Sebastian Pranz/Archive of Transition
131
Fabian Weiss/Archive of Transition
132
Personal archive Giorgi Eliava Institute
for Bacteriophages
133
Fabian Weiss/Archive of Transition
134-135
Fabian Weiss/Archive of Transition

138-145
Mamuka Japharidze
155-165
Fabian Weiss/Archive of Transition
170-175
Nukri Jioshvili/personal archive
Gela Kuprashvili
185,188,189,191
Fabian Weiss/Archive of Transition
196-203
Personal archive Nana Kalandarishvili
206-207
National Archives of Georgia
209
Personal archive Nana Kalandarishvili
214-215
Merab Bolqvadze
for detailed information, see:
http://maps.tbilisi.gov.ge/

Imprint

The Deutsche Nationalbibliothek lists this publication in the Deutsche Nationalbibliografie; detailed bibliographic data are available on the Internet at dnb.dnb.de

Tbilisi – Archive of Transition
ISBN 978-3-7212-0983-9
© 2018 niggli, imprint of Braun Publishing AG, Salenstein
www.niggli.ch

1st edition 2018

Editors
Klaus Neuburg, Sebastian Pranz, Lexo Soselia, Wato Tsereteli, Jesse Vogler, Fabian Weiss

Art Director
Simon Roth

Design Concept and Layout
Laurens Bauer, Lukas Esser

Translators
Irina Abulashvili (Georgian to English), Tornike Khomeriki (Georgian to English), Ben Knight (German to English)

Proofreader
Ben Knight

Copy Editor
Nele Kröger (niggli)

Typography
Akzidenz-Grotesk BQ

Postproduction
Bild1Druck GmbH

Printed in the European Union

Realization

FROH!

CENTER OF CONTEMPORARY ART-TBILISI

Among the many people who helped with this project we especially like to thank Stephan Wackwitz, who brought this group together in the first place.

We also thank our patrons Michael Birgden and Sascha König, Claus Hipp, Christian Jacobs, Peter Mönnig and all the people who supported this project in our crowdfunding campaign.

Many thanks to
Michael Basseler, Alisa Blatter, Markus Sebastian Braun, Rusudan Chkhikvishvili, Erekle Eko Chakhvashvili, Irine Chogoshvili, Maia Danelia, Nona Davitaia, Judith Dörrenbächer, Nino Dzandzava, Galaqtion Eristavi, Mirjam Flender, Tamta Gochitashvili, Stephan Goetz, Mamuka Japharidze, Tornike Jashia, Nana Kalandarishvili, Levan Kalandarishvili, Mako Kapanadze, Kati Krause, Tinatin Khomeriki, Klasse Grafik of the HBFK Hamburg, Matthias Klingenberg, Tako Kobakhidze, Boris Kochan, Gela Kuprashvili, Nino Lejava, Tamara Lortkipanidze, Ryan McCarrel, Medea Metreveli, Liisi Mölder, Horst Moser, Bessie Normand, Ingo Offermanns, Tatiana Remneva, Giorgi Rodionov, Mariam Shevardnadze, Sophie Steybe, Rafael Tkhuvaleli, Zura Tsofurashvili, Barbara von Münchhausen, Jeannette Weber

The book was published as part of the program honoring Georgia as the Guest of Honor country at the 2018 Frankfurter Buchmesse with the support of the Georgian National Book Center and the Ministry of Culture and Sport of Georgia.

Partners

Federal Foreign Office

GEORGIAN NATIONAL BOOK CENTER

Washington University in St. Louis

HEINRICH BÖLL STIFTUNG SOUTH CAUCASUS

GOETHE INSTITUT

NATIONAL ARCHIVES OF GEORGIA

vhs
DVV International

H F B K

MINISTRY OF CULTURE AND SPORT OF GEORGIA

Georgia
Made by Characters